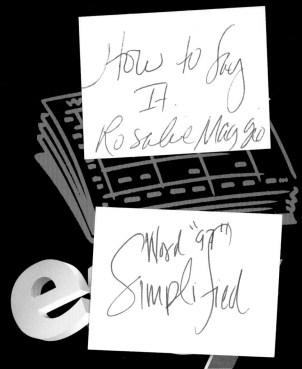

How to Say It. Rosalie Maggio

Word "97"
Simplified

Microsoft®
Excel 2000

See it done

Do it yourself

que®

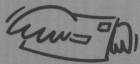

Copyright© 1999 by Que® Corporation

Library of Congress Catalog No.: 98-87063

ISBN: 0-7897-1867-7

01 00 99   6 5 4 3 2

Interpretation of the printing code: the rightmost double-digit number is the year of the book's printing; the rightmost single-digit number, the number of the book's printing. For example, a printing code of 99-1 shows that the first printing of the book occurred in 1999.

Printed in the United States of America

About the Author

Nancy Warner is a private consultant in the computer and publishing arenas currently focusing on freelance writing and development editing. She graduated from Purdue University in Computer Information Systems and has worked as an end user specialist, data access analyst, product development specialist, and marketing manager. Along with the numerous computer books she has developed and edited, she has written or contributed to *Easy Office 2000, Excel 2000 Quick Ref, Word 2000 Quick Ref, Office 2000 Quick Ref, Easy Office 97 Second Edition, Special Edition Using Office 97 Platinum Edition, Sams Teach Yourself Office 97 in 10 Minutes, Easy Windows NT Workstation 4.0,* and *How to Use Access 97*. Currently she lives in Arizona with her pug dog, Pudgy.

Acknowledgments

I would like to thank Jamie Milazzo for working with me on this project and always making me laugh. In addition, a special thanks to Linda Seifert for her dedication and hard work.

Dedication

To Sid, thanks for betting against Purdue, even though we both won! ;-)

Executive Editor
Angela Wethington

Acquisitions Editor
Jamie Milazzo

Development Editor
Nancy D. Warner

Technical Editor
Michelle Heilman

Managing Editor
Thomas F. Hayes

Project Editor
Linda Seifert

Copy Editor
Jill Bond

Indexer
Greg Pearson

Proofreader
Tricia Sterling

Production Team
Trina Wurst

Illustrations
Bruce Dean

How to Use This Book

It's as Easy as 1-2-3

Each part of this book is made up of a series of short, instructional lessons, designed to help you understand basic information that you need to get the most out of your computer hardware and software.

Click: Click the left mouse button once.

Double-click: Click the left mouse button twice in rapid succession.

Right-click: Click the right mouse button once.

Pointer Arrow: Highlights an item on the screen you need to point to or focus on in the step or task.

Selection: Highlights the area onscreen discussed in the step or task.

Click & Type: Click once where indicated and begin typing to enter your text or data.

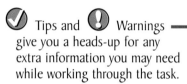

Tips and ① **Warnings** give you a heads-up for any extra information you may need while working through the task.

2 Each task includes a series of quick, easy steps designed to guide you through the procedure.

1 Each step is fully illustrated to show you how it looks onscreen.

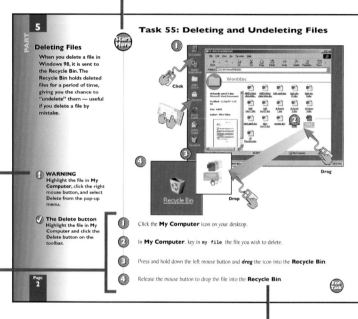

Task 55: Deleting and Undeleting Files

Deleting Files
When you delete a file in Windows 98, it is sent to the Recycle Bin. The Recycle Bin holds deleted files for a period of time, giving you the chance to "undelete" them — useful if you delete a file by mistake.

① **WARNING**
Highlight the file in **My Computer**, click the right mouse button, and select Delete from the pop-up menu.

✓ **The Delete button**
Highlight the file in My Computer and click the Delete button on the toolbar.

1 Click the **My Computer** icon on your desktop.

2 In **My Computer**, key in my `file` the file you wish to delete.

3 Press and hold down the left mouse button and **drag** the icon into the **Recycle Bin**.

4 Release the mouse button to drop the file into the **Recycle Bin**.

3 Items that you select or click in menus, dialog boxes, tabs, and windows are shown in **Bold**. Information you type is in a **special font**.

How to Drag: Point to the starting place or object. Hold down the mouse button (right or left per instructions), move the mouse to the new location, then release the button.

Next Step: If you see this symbol, it means the task you're working on continues on the next page.

End Task: Task is complete.

Introduction to Microsoft Excel 2000

If you've picked up this book, you probably use or are thinking of using Excel either in your home or business. Excel is the best-selling spreadsheet program available, and with it, you can create all kinds of financial documents—budgets, sales worksheets, income totals, expense reports, loan payments, and more. If there's something you need to do with numbers, Excel is the program for that job.

But Excel isn't your *life*. You don't want to learn every little function and feature. You want the basics, enough to get your job done as quickly and painlessly as possible. That's why this book is perfect for you.

Easy Excel 2000 provides concise, visual, step-by-step instructions for all the key tasks. You can *see* how to perform each task. The book covers the most common things you do and covers the best way to do them. You learn how to create, edit, format, and print worksheets. You also learn how to jazz up a worksheet with charts, pictures, links to Web sites, and more. As an added bonus, you can use Excel as a mini-database program; this book also covers the database features of Excel. And finally, you learn how to make some changes to how the program works. Just about everything you need in one *easy* book.

You can turn to a particular task and follow the steps for that task. You can read the book from cover to cover. You can use the book as a reference. You can turn to a particular topic (like charts) and follow all the tasks for that topic. No matter how you use it, you will find the information you need to make learning Excel easy.

Getting Started

To learn any new **application**, it's a good idea to have some basic knowledge of how to start the application, what appears onscreen, how to ask for help, and how to exit the application. If you are new to Excel, read this part so that you get a good understanding of these basic skills. If you have used Excel before, you may want to skim through this part to see what's new in the 2000 version.

A **worksheet** is a grid of **columns** and **rows**. The intersection of any column and row is called a **cell**. Each cell in a worksheet has a unique cell reference, the designation formed by combining the row and column headings. For example, A8 refers to the cell at the intersection of column A and row 8.

The **cell pointer** is a white cross-shaped pointer that appears over cells in the worksheet. You use the cell pointer to select any cell in the worksheet. The selected cell is called the **active cell**. You always have at least one cell selected at all times.

A **range** is a specified group of cells. A range can be a single cell, a column, a row, or any combination of cells, columns, and rows. Range coordinates identify a range. The first element in the range coordinates is the location of the upper left cell in the range; the second element is the location of the lower-right cell. A colon (:) separates these two elements. The range AI:C3, for example, includes the cells AI, A2, A3, BI, B2, B3, CI, C2, and C3. The following topics are covered:

Tasks

Task 1: Starting Excel

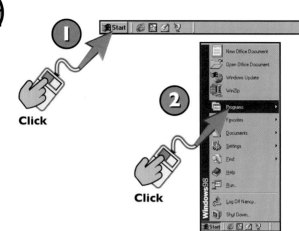

Opening the Excel Application

When you install Excel, the installation program sets up the necessary program files and folders, including adding a program icon to the Start menu. To start the application, click the Microsoft Excel command.

✓ **Starting an Application from a File**

Another way to start the Excel application is to double-click a saved workbook file, for example, in a Windows 98 Explorer window. Windows automatically starts the application and opens the workbook you selected.

✓ **Locating the Excel Icon**

If you have rearranged your Start menu and placed Excel someplace else, open that program folder first, then click the program icon.

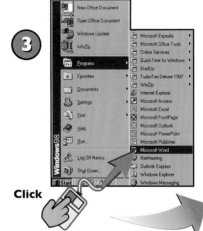

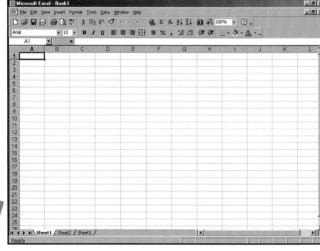

1 Click the **Start** menu.

2 Click the **Programs** command.

3 Click **Microsoft Excel** and a blank worksheet appears onscreen.

Task 2: Moving Around in a Workbook

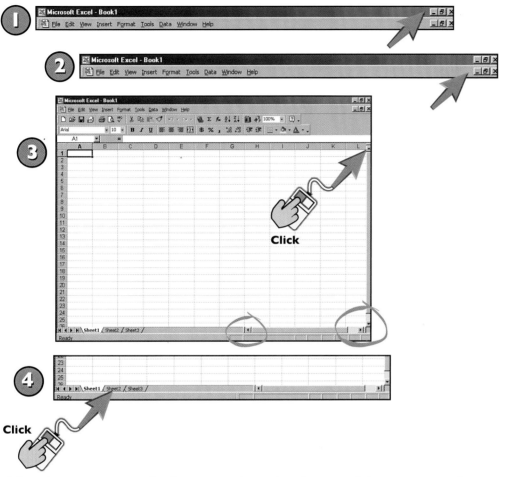

Click

Click

Understanding the Excel Workspace

On your desk, you probably have tools such as pens, a notepad, stapler, and so on, within reach. Just like your physical desk, Excel puts a lot of tools close by on your electronic desk. You can use these tools to change the size of the windows, select commands, get information, and more.

1. Select the **program window** controls to alter the size of the program window.

2. Select the **document window** controls to alter the size of the document window.

3. Click the **arrows** on the scrollbars to scroll in that direction or drag the scroll box up, down, left, or right.

4. Click the **sheet tabs** at the bottom left of the workbook to move between worksheets.

✓ Hiding the Status Bar

If you decide you want more room for the worksheet area, you can hide the Status bar or Formula bar. Open the **View** menu and then uncheck the items you want to turn off (**Formula Bar** or **Status Bar**). In addition, **View, Full Screen** displays only the menu bar, screen, and worksheets tabs.

End Task

Task 3: Understanding the Worksheet Area

Learning Parts of a Worksheet

Rows are numbered (1, 2, 3, and so on), and columns are lettered (A, B, C, and so on). The intersection of a row and column is a *cell* with a *cell reference* (A1, B2, C3, and so on). The cell with a black border is the *active cell*. The active cell has a light blue background so that you can easily see the data in the cell.

✓ Shortcuts

You can select an entire worksheet by simultaneously pressing **Ctrl+A**. You can immediately move to the beginning of the worksheet by simultaneously pressing **Ctrl+Home**.

✓ Go To a Specific Cell

If you need to go to a specific cell, you can choose **Edit, Go To** and list the cell name or cell address, and Excel immediately takes you to the cell reference and makes it the active cell. For more information, see Part 2, Task 13 "Going to a Particular Cell," for more information.

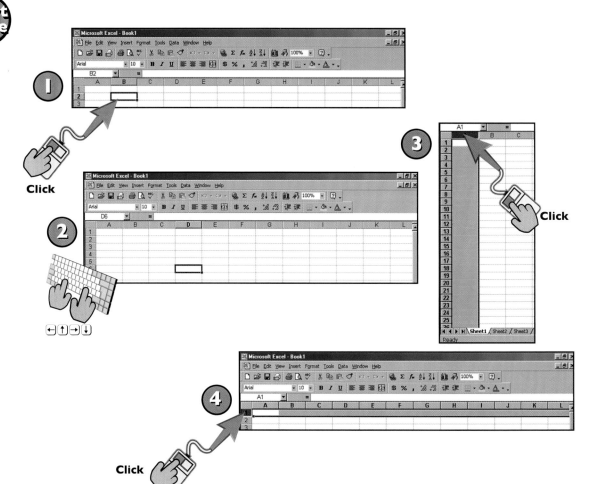

Start Here

Click

Click

Click

Click

1. Click a cell, which makes it the active cell. The active cell has a black border and the cell reference is listed in the formula bar (for example, **B2**).

2. Press the arrow keys to get the feel of how you can move from cell to cell.

3. Click a column header to select an entire column (for example, **A**).

4. Click a row header to select an entire row (for example, **1**).

End Task

Task 4: Entering Data

Start Here

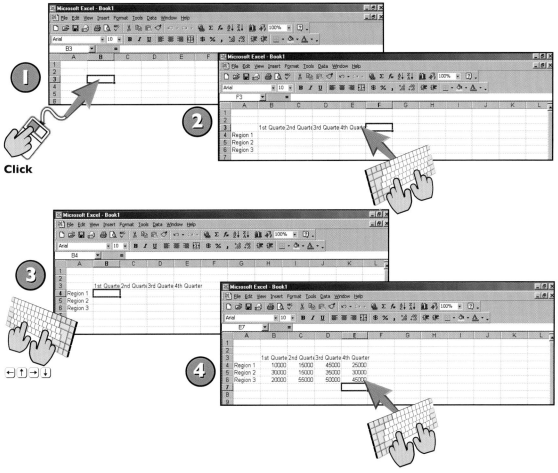

Click

Typing Data in Cells

A data entry into a worksheet can contain text or any combination of numbers and text. You can enter data into a blank worksheet or add data to an existing worksheet that already contains some data. Notice that the status bar displays Enter when you are typing data into a cell. This tells you that the cell is active and you are currently entering information.

1. Click the cell in which you want to begin adding data (for example, **B3**).

2. Type some text into a few different cells and press the arrow keys to move to the next cell below (for example, row headers and column headers).

3. Press the arrow keys on the keyboard to move to different cells.

4. Type some numbers into a few different cells to fill out the table.

✓ Typing Errors

If you make a mistake while you are typing, you can press the Backspace key to remove the incorrect information, then type the correct information. You will learn more about editing and deleting data in Part 3 "Editing Worksheets."

End Task

Task 5: Selecting Cells

Choosing a Cell and a Range of Cells

The Excel worksheet contains thousands of rows and columns. You probably won't use that much space, but you do need a way to move around within the area of the worksheet you will use. You can easily move from cell to cell. When you want to select an individual cell, you just click it. But, there will be times when you want to work on a group of cells.

A group of cells is called a range, and you can easily select a range of cells next to each other. What happens if the cells you want to select aren't next to each other? Suppose that you want to select some cells in column A and some in column E. You aren't limited to selecting cells next to each other, this is known as a **noncontiguous range**.

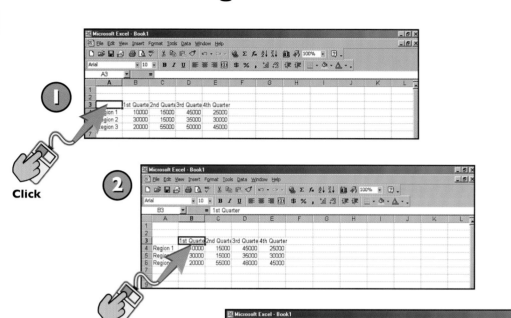

Start Here

① **Click**

② **Click**

③ **Drag** **Drop**

① Click the cell you want to make active (for example, **A3**). A thick black border indicates the active cell.

② Click on the cell that you want to be the first cell in a range of cells (for example, **B3**).

③ Press and hold down the left mouse button while you drag the pointer over the cells and release the mouse button at cell **E3**. The range of cells appears in a light blue color, and the first cell remains white.

Next Step

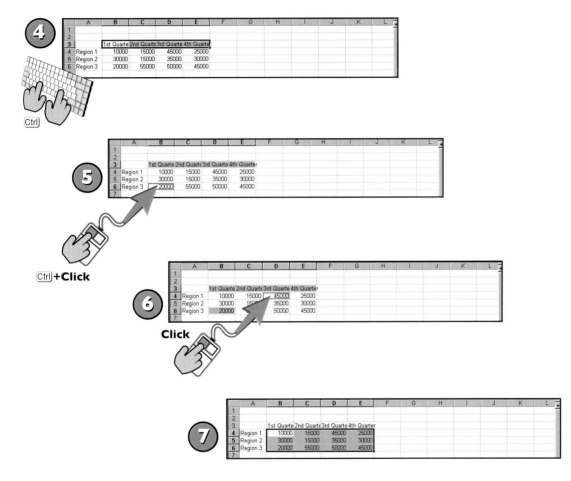

Keyboard Shortcuts
You can also use the keyboard to select cells:

Press	To select...
Shift+→	Right one cell
Shift+←	Left one cell
Shift+↓	Down one cell
Shift+↑	Up one cell
Ctrl+A	All cells

Range References
A range is indicated with a range reference, which includes the upper-leftmost cell, a colon, and the lower-rightmost cell. For example, G2 through G9 would actually appear G2:G9.

Try Again
To deselect a group or range of cells, release the Ctrl key and click outside of the selected cells. If you click a cell that you didn't want in the selection, you need to start selecting the cells all over again.

4 Press the **Ctrl** key on the keyboard while the range is selected onscreen. The Ctrl key continues your selection.

5 Click cell **B6** while continuing to press the **Ctrl** key.

6 Click cell **D4** and release the **Ctrl** key.

7 Select another range of cells (for example, **B4** through **E6**) while pressing the **Ctrl** key. (Refer to steps 2 and 3 if you need help selecting a range.)

Working with Regular and Personalized Menus

The menu bar is just below the title bar and varies from application to application. You select commands on the menu to perform operations such as saving a file, formatting text, or printing a document. *Personalized menus* are a new feature in **Office 2000.** Personalized menus change depending on what you are trying to accomplish in the application. They hide infrequently used commands so it's easier for you to find the ones you use a lot. In addition, if you have personalized menus turned on, every time you execute a command that's on the *hidden* portion of the personalized menu, it becomes one of the commonly available commands.

Task 6: Working with Menus

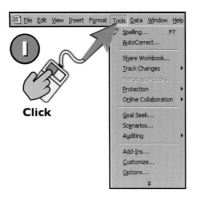

Click

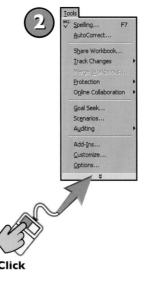

Click

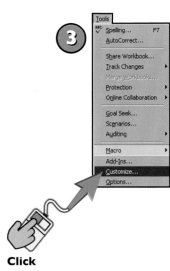

Click

Click **Tools** in the menu bar, which opens the personalized Tools menu.

Click the double-down arrow at the bottom of the menu to expand the menu.

Click the **Customize** command on the Tools menu.

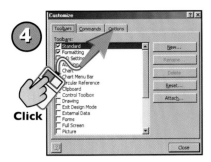

Click

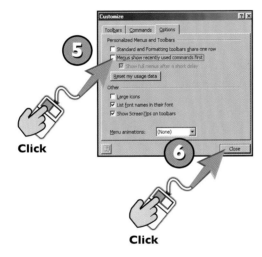

Click

Click

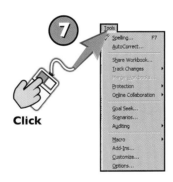

Click

Menu Options
You can access any option on a menu unless the option is grayed out, which means the option is not available for the action you want to perform.

Closing a Menu
To close a menu without making a selection, click on the menu name again, click outside the menu, or press the Esc key.

Short Delay
Another option on the Customize dialog box, Options tab, is **Show full menus after a short delay.** If you uncheck this option, you must click the double-down arrow on a personalized menu instead of just moving the mouse pointer over the double-down arrow.

Customizing Menus
Keep in mind that you must set your customized menu options in each Office application. Changing the defaults in one location doesn't apply to other Office applications. The Customize dialog box can be accessed in each application the same way: choose **Tools, Customize.**

---

④ Click the **Options** tab on the Customize dialog box.

⑤ Uncheck the **Menus show recently used commands first** option under the **Personalized Menus and Toolbars** section.

⑥ Click the **Close** button to close the dialog box.

⑦ Click **Tools** in the menu bar, which opens the complete Tools menu.

Working with the Standard and Formatting Toolbars

Excel includes two toolbars, each with a set of toolbar buttons. You can use the buttons as a shortcut for selecting commonly used commands. The top toolbar is called the Standard toolbar, and the next toolbar is called the Formatting toolbar.

✓ **Toolbar Options**

Keep in mind that you must set your customized toolbar options in each **Office application. Changing** the defaults in one location doesn't apply to other **Office applications. But you** access the **Customize** dialog box in each application the same way: choose **Tools, Customize.**

Task 7: Working with Toolbars

Start Here

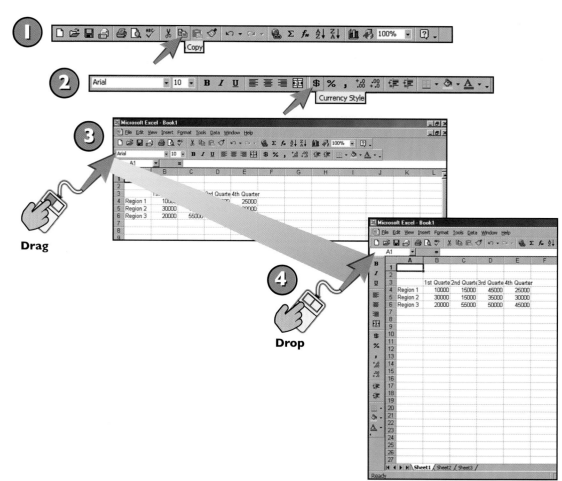

Copy

Currency Style

Drag

Drop

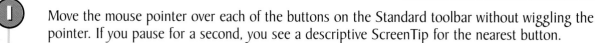

1 Move the mouse pointer over each of the buttons on the Standard toolbar without wiggling the pointer. If you pause for a second, you see a descriptive ScreenTip for the nearest button.

2 Move the mouse pointer over each of the buttons on the Formatting toolbar without wiggling the pointer. If you pause for a second, you see a descriptive ScreenTip for the nearest button.

3 Click and hold down the left mouse button on the vertical bar on the leftmost side of the Formatting toolbar, and drag the toolbar somewhere on your desktop.

4 Release the mouse button to drop the toolbar in its new location (for example, on the left side of the window).

Next Step

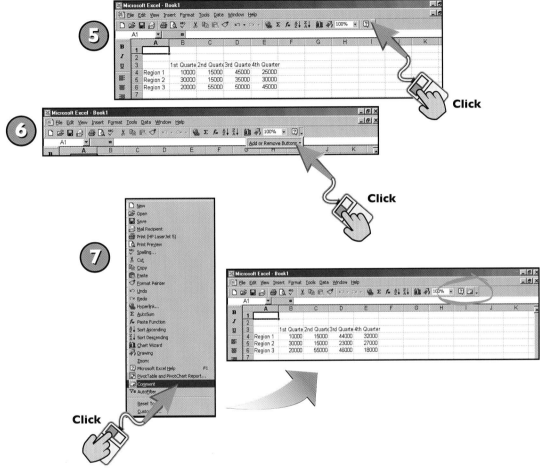

5 Click the **More Buttons** down arrow on the rightmost side of the Standard toolbar.

6 Click the **Add or Remove Buttons** command.

7 Click the command button you would like to add or remove from the Standard toolbar (for example, add the **Comment** button), and it will appear on the toolbar.

Customizing Toolbars
If the command button you want to add to your toolbar isn't located in the More Buttons drop-down list, click the Customize command. Click the Commands tab on the Customize dialog box and scroll through the categories and commands. Click the command you want to add to your toolbar, drag and drop it directly on the toolbar, and close the dialog box.

WARNING
Be careful not to accidentally eliminate commands and options that you use frequently. If you want the toolbar set to the original default commands, choose **More Buttons, Add or Remove Buttons, Reset Toolbar.**

Using Shortcut Menus

When you right-click an item in your workspace, a *shortcut menu* appears (also known as a *pop-up* or *context menu*). Shortcut menus include the commands you use most for whatever is currently selected—text, cells, charts, pictures, and so on. The shortcut menu commands vary, depending on your selection. For example, you might use a shortcut menu instead of a toolbar to quickly edit or format data.

Task 8: Using the Right Mouse Button

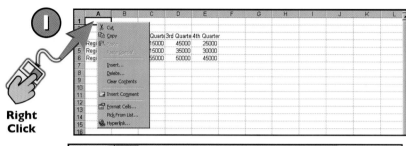

Right Click

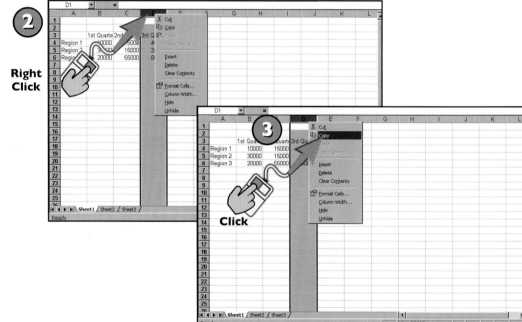

Right Click

Click

✓ Closing a Shortcut Menu

Sometimes you display a shortcut menu that doesn't have the command you want to use. To leave a shortcut menu without making a selection, press the **Esc** key or click elsewhere on the desktop.

1 Right-click a cell to see the shortcut menu.

2 Right-click a different object (for example, a column or row) to see the shortcut menu.

3 Click a command on the shortcut menu (for example, **Copy**). The action is performed and the shortcut menu disappears.

Task 9: Getting Help from the Office Assistant

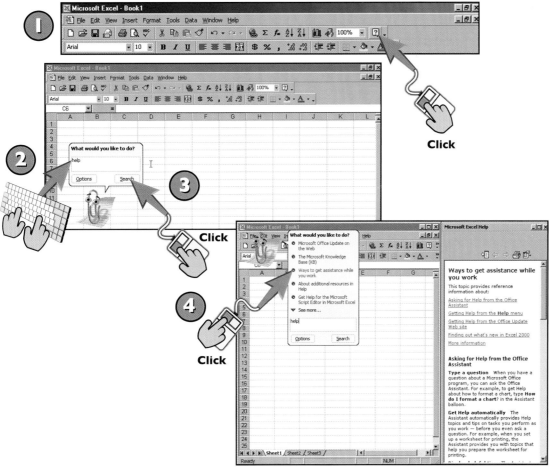

Click

Click

Click

Using the Office Assistant

You can also use the **Office Assistant** to get help. You can ask a question, and the Assistant will display relevant help topics. You can turn on the **Assistant** at any time. You may also see the Assistant pop up when you perform certain tasks; the Assistant then will ask whether you want help with what you are doing.

 Closing the Assistant
When you finish reading the Help information, click the **X** in the upper-right corner of the Help window to close the window. If you don't want to use the Office Assistant, you can turn it off and use the regular Office 2000 help. Right-click the **Assistant** and choose **Options**. Uncheck the **Use the Office Assistant** option and click the **OK** button. Then you can start regular Help by clicking the **Help** button.

1. Click the **Office Assistant** button on the Standard toolbar (or click the Assistant itself if it is already visible).

2. Type the topic or question you want help on; for example, type **help** in the text box.

3. Click the **Search** button to view the list of Help topics.

4. Click the Help topic you want information on. The Help window appears with information about the topic you selected.

 End Task

Task 10: Looking Up Help from the Index

Getting Index Help

If you don't want to scan the table of contents, you can use Excel's online help index to get help. You can type the word or phrase you want to find and then view a list of all matching topics. You can view an indexed list or search for the topic.

✓ **Closing Help**
When you are done reviewing the help information, click the **Close (X)** button.

✓ **Underlined Terms**
If a word or phrase is underlined, it means that you can display a pop-up definition for the term. Point to the term and click the mouse button. A definition appears.

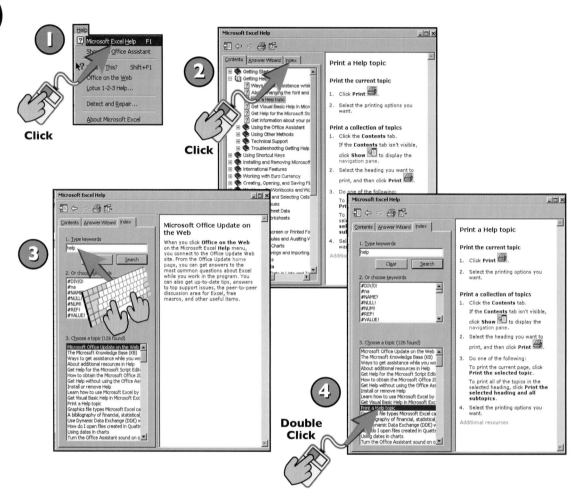

Start Here

Click

Click

Double Click

1. Choose **Help**, **Microsoft Excel Help** to open Microsoft Excel Help.

2. Click the **Index** tab.

3. Type the keywords you want to find (for example, **help**) and press the **Enter** key.

4. Double-click the topic you want help with and you will see the relevant help information in the help window to the right (for example, **Print a Help topic**).

End Task

Task 11: Getting Help Using the Contents Tab

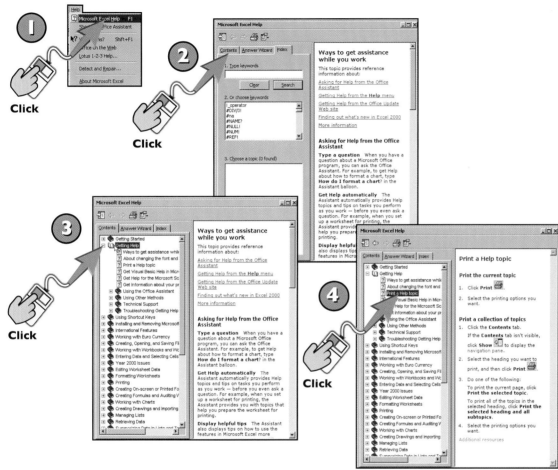

Start Here

Click

Click

Click

Click

Working with Excel Help

If you can't remember how to perform a task, use Excel's online help system to remind you how. The online help system offers many ways to get help. One way is to use the **Contents** tab, which is similar to using the table of contents of a book. When you use this command, Excel displays a list of topics. You select the topic you want, and Excel displays additional subtopics. You continue selecting topics until you find the information you want.

✅ **Closing Help**
When you are done reviewing the help information, click the **Close (X)** button.

✅ **Printing Topics**
To print the how-to information, click the **Print** button. To go back to a previous topic, click the **Back** button.

1. Choose **Help**, **Microsoft Excel Help** to open Microsoft Excel Help.

2. Click the **Contents** tab.

3. Click the **+** sign to the left of the topic (for example, **Getting Help**) and the list expands to show subtopics.

4. Click any of these subtopics (for example, **Print a Help topic**) and you see the relevant information in the help window to the right.

End Task

Task 12: Asking Excel What's This?

Start Here

Using What's This? Help

There will be times when a ScreenTip of a command doesn't give you enough information for you to know what the command does. Or you don't want to search for the information in Help, but you would like to know what the command is for. Excel 2000 gives you the What's This? option for these situations. It also gives you the What's This? option when you are in a dialog box and cannot use the Help menu.

✓ **What's This? in a Dialog Box**
If you are unsure of an option in a dialog box, you can click the ? button to the left of the **Close (X)** button. You can then click the option to activate a What's This? pop up.

✓ **Using What's This? Fast**
You can simultaneously press the **Shift+F1** shortcut keys to activate the What's This? option.

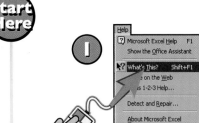

Click

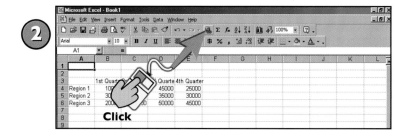

Click

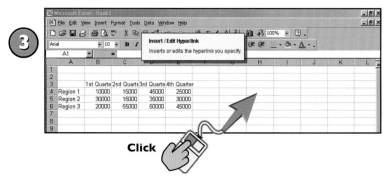

Click

1 Choose **Help**, **What's This?**

2 Click the command or object you want explained (for example, the **Insert Hyperlink** button) and read the What's This? pop up.

3 Click anywhere in your workspace to clear the pop-up information.

End Task

Task 13: Exiting Excel

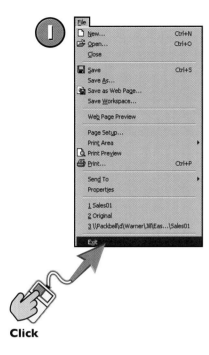

Click

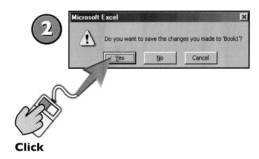

Click

Closing the Excel Application

When you are finished working on your worksheet, you can save the worksheet and exit Excel. You should always save your worksheets and save often (more on saving in Part 3). You also should exit the program when you are done, so that you save your system resources.

① Choose **File, Exit** and the application closes. If you are working in a document and have not yet saved your work, the application asks you to save.

② Click the **Yes** button if you want to save your work, the **No** button if you don't want to save your work, or the **Cancel** button if you want to return to the document without saving or exiting.

✅ **Exit Shortcut**
Press the **Alt+F4** key combination to select the File, Exit command.

✅ **Shut Down Windows**
To shut down Windows, click the **Start** button and then select **Shut Down**. Select **Shut down the computer** and click **OK**.

PART 2

Managing and Viewing Workbooks

As you continue to work in Excel you will learn how important it is to save your work and access workbook files. You should save often, and you also should spend some time keeping your documents organized. In addition, multiple worksheets help you organize, manage, and consolidate your data. For example, you might want to create a sales forecast for the first quarter of the year. Sheet1, Sheet2, and Sheet3 could contain worksheet data for January, February, and March; Sheet4 a summary for the three months of sales data; and Sheet5 a chart showing sales over the three-month period.

Tasks

Storing Your Work on Disk

Until you save a workbook, all your work is vulnerable. The information is stored only temporarily in memory. It is good practice to regularly save your workbooks as you work. After you save a workbook, you can retrieve it later. The first time you save the workbook, you are prompted for a filename and a folder.

✓ Save In Option

If you don't want to save your file in the **My Documents** directory, you can select the **Save in** drop-down list box and maneuver through your folders to save the file in a different location.

✓ Save Button

If you have already named the file, you can click on the **Save** button on the Standard toolbar to quickly save your recent changes.

Task 1: Saving a Workbook

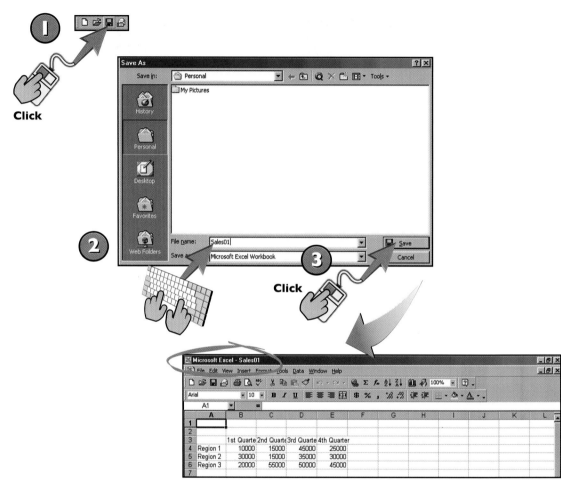

Start Here

Click

Click

Click

1. Click the **Save** button on the Standard toolbar.

2. Type a different filename if you want (for example, **Sales01**) in the Save As dialog box.

3. Click the **Save** button in the Save As dialog box. The title bar now contains your workbook's name.

End Task

Task 2: Closing a Workbook

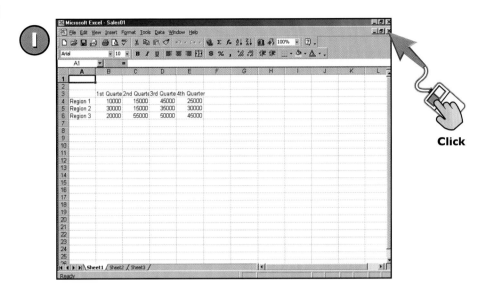

Click

Click

Finishing with a Workbook

When you finish working on a workbook, you can close it and continue to work in the application. You can close a workbook with or without saving changes. If you have been working in a workbook and you try to close it, Excel asks you whether you want to save the workbook before it closes.

1. Click the **Close** button on the menu bar. If you have made any changes to the workbook, Excel asks you to save the workbook.

2. Click the **Yes** button if you want to save changes; click the **No** button to close Excel without saving changes; click **Cancel** if you want to return to the workbook. Excel then closes the workbook.

✓ Buttons Available
When Excel has no workbooks open, only a few buttons are available on the Standard toolbar. Notice that as soon as you create a new workbook (see Task 3) or open a workbook (see Task 4), the buttons are available again.

Task 3: Creating a New Workbook

Adding a Workbook

Excel presents a new blank workbook each time you start the program. You can create another new workbook at any time, however. For example, when you save and close one workbook, you might want to begin a new one.

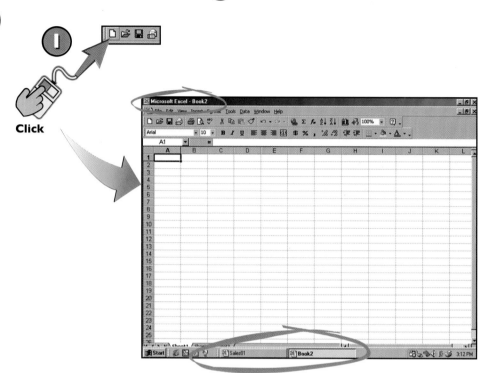

Start Here

1

Click

✓ **Default Filenames**

The default filename for each new workbook (Book1, Book2, Book3, and so on) automatically increases sequentially. If you exit and start Excel again, the numbers begin at 1 again.

1 Click the **New** button on the standard toolbar. Excel opens a new workbook with A1 as the active cell.

End Task

Task 4: Opening a Workbook

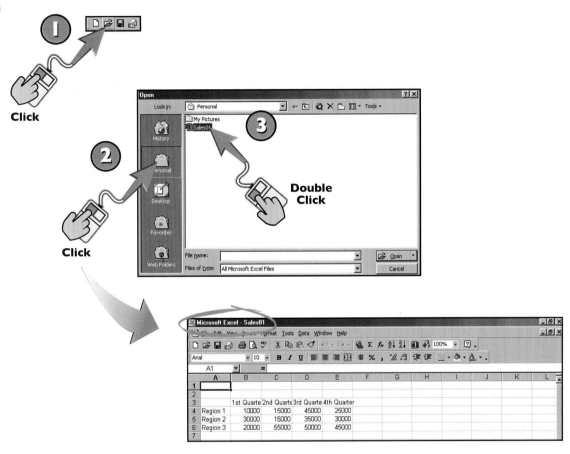

Click

Click

Double Click

Start Here

Retrieving a Workbook from Disk

Each time you want to work with an Excel workbook, you need to open it. You have many options from which to choose in the Open dialog box. If necessary, click the **Look In** drop-down arrow and select a folder from the list. To move up a folder level, click the **Up One Level** button on the Open toolbar. If you double-click a subfolder, its contents appear in the **Files and Folders** list.

✓ Change Dialog Box Views

You can view different information about the files in the Open dialog box (and the **Save As** dialog box in Task 4) by clicking on the **Views** button on the dialog box's toolbar.

✓ Opening Recent Files

Click **File** to display a list of recently opened and saved files that appear at the bottom of the File menu.

1 Click the **Open** button on the standard toolbar.

2 Click the **Personal** icon on the Places bar (your icon might say **My Documents** instead), or wherever you save your workbooks.

3 Double-click the file you want to open in the Open dialog box (for example, **Sales01**) and Excel opens the workbook.

Task 5: Viewing Multiple Workbooks

Seeing Several Workbooks on the Screen

Instead of constantly switching between workbooks, you can view multiple workbooks onscreen in Excel. This is a convenient feature if you are comparing two workbooks or working on two workbooks at the same time. You can have more than two workbooks open at a time, and you can also resize their windows. The workbook displaying a darker title bar is considered the active workbook. The active cell is visible in the active workbook.

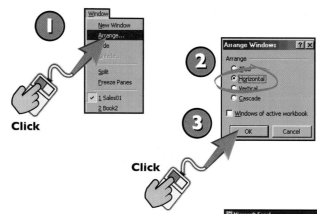

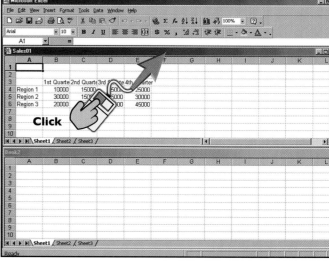

✓ **Maximizing One Workbook**
To return to viewing only one workbook (maximizing the workbook), double-click on the title bar of the workbook in which you want to work.

 Choose **Window**, **Arrange** to open the Arrange Windows dialog box.

 Select how you want the windows arranged (for example, **Horizontal**).

 Click the **OK** button.

 Click on the title bar or in the body of the workbook you want to work in to make it the active worksheet.

Task 6: Switching Between Workbooks

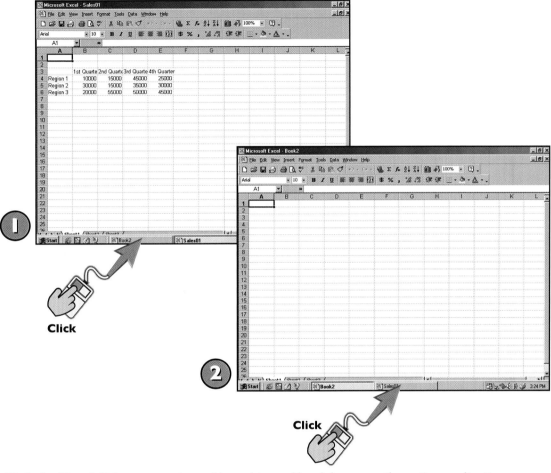

Click

Click

Moving Between Open Workbooks

You can have multiple workbooks open at the same time and switch between them whenever you want. For example, you might be using two different workbooks to create one report. You can use the Windows taskbar to quickly move from one workbook to another or to a completely different Office application.

① ** Click the **Book2 button on the taskbar; this workbook becomes the active application and workbook.

② ** Click the **Sales01 button on the taskbar; this workbook becomes the active application and workbook.

✔ Resizing Application Windows

If your application windows aren't maximized, you can resize them to view multiple windows on the desktop. Do this by placing the mouse pointer on the window border, where the pointer turns into a double-headed arrow. Then click the left mouse button and drag the window to the desired size.

Task 7: Switching Between Worksheets

Viewing Different Worksheets

In addition to having multiple workbooks open at a time and switching between them whenever you want, you can have data and information stored on separate worksheets within a single workbook. For example, you might want to keep Product Sales data for different years on separate worksheets.

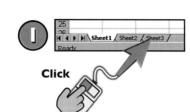

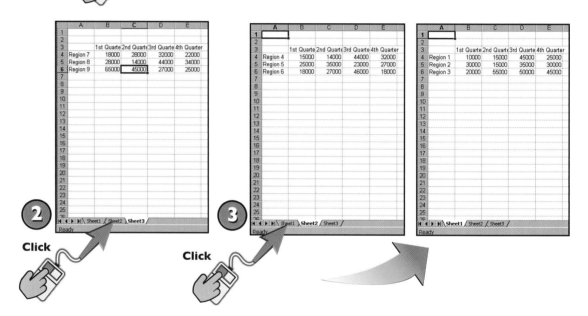

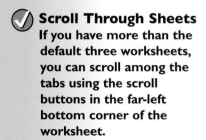

Scroll Through Sheets
If you have more than the default three worksheets, you can scroll among the tabs using the scroll buttons in the far-left bottom corner of the worksheet.

① Click the **Sheet3** tab to see the contents in the worksheet.

② Click the **Sheet2** tab to see the contents in the worksheet.

③ Click the **Sheet1** tab to see the contents in the worksheet.

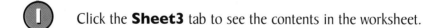

End Task

Task 8: Naming Worksheets

Start Here

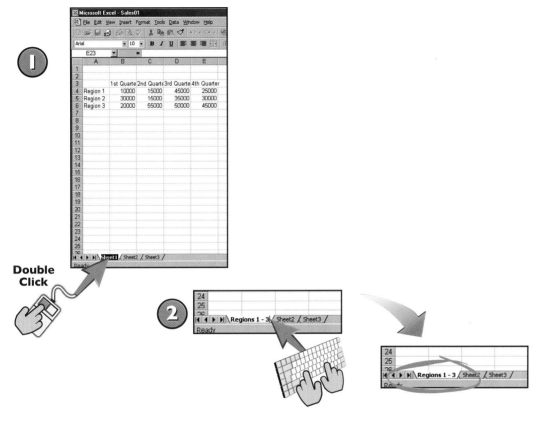

Double Click

Assigning Sheet Titles

The default names, Sheet1, Sheet2, and so on, aren't all that descriptive. If you use several sheets in a workbook, you should rename them so that you know what each sheet contains. Naming makes switching from one worksheet to another easier, too.

✓ Save Workbook Names

Don't confuse worksheet names with workbook (file) names. They aren't the same. You still need to name and save the workbook, as described in Part 2, Task 1 "Saving a Workbook."

✓ Scroll Through Tabs

If you have several worksheets, you can scroll among the tabs using the scroll buttons in the left-bottom corner of the worksheet.

① Double-click the sheet tab of the sheet you want to rename (for example, **Sheet1**). The current name is highlighted.

② Type the new name (for example, **Regions 1 – 3**) and press the **Enter** key. Excel displays the new name on the worksheet tab.

End Task

Task 9: Inserting a Worksheet

Adding Another Worksheet

A new workbook by default includes three sheets. You can easily add more sheets, if needed. You might, for example, use a worksheet for each quarter of yearly sales and one for the total. In this example, you need five worksheets. You can add the other worksheets.

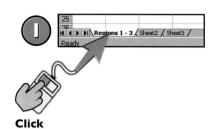

Click

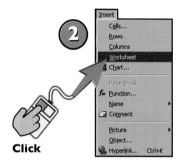

Click

✓ **Using the Shortcut Menu**
You also name a worksheet by using the shortcut menu. Point to a sheet tab and click the right mouse button. Then, click the command you want.

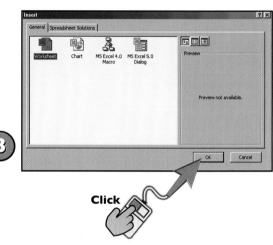

Click

✓ **Copy or Move a Worksheet**
To move a worksheet, click the sheet tab and then drag the tab to the new location. To copy a worksheet, hold down the Ctrl key and drag the tab to the new location.

 Click *before* the worksheet in which you want to insert the new worksheet.

 Choose **Insert**, **Worksheet**. Excel inserts a new blank worksheet. This new worksheet is selected.

 Click the **OK** button on the Insert dialog box to insert a new worksheet.

Task 10: Deleting a Worksheet

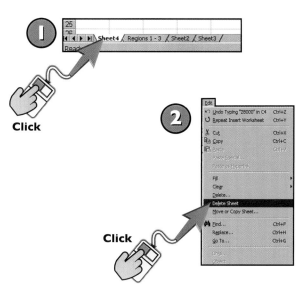

Click

Click

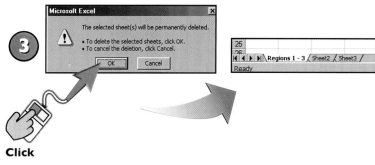

Click

Removing a Worksheet

If you don't want extra sheets in your worksheet, you can delete them. Remember that Excel deletes not only the sheet, but all the data on that sheet. For this reason, you are prompted to confirm the deletion. Be sure that you don't delete sheets that contain information you need.

① Click the sheet you want to delete (for example, **Sheet4**).

② Choose **Edit**, **Delete Sheet**.

③ Click the **OK** button to confirm the deletion. The worksheet and all its data is deleted.

⚠ WARNING
You cannot undo the action of deleting a worksheet. Make sure you have a backup copy of the workbook or are positive that you will never need the worksheet again.

✓ Delete a Worksheet
To delete a worksheet quickly, right-click the sheet you want to delete and choose Delete from the shortcut menu.

Using a Worksheet Structure

When you are organizing your workbooks, you might need to do a little rearranging. You might, for example, want to use the same basic structure of one worksheet in another workbook. Rather than duplicate your efforts, you can copy a worksheet to another workbook. To start, be sure both workbooks are open.

Task 11: Copying a Worksheet to Another Workbook

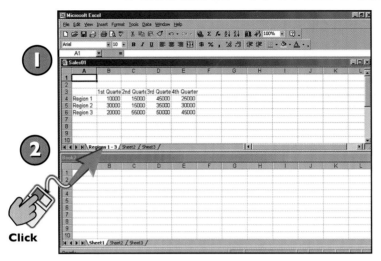

Click

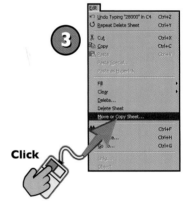
Click

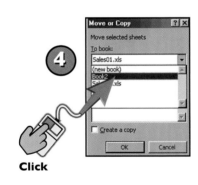
Click

✓ **Moving a Worksheet**
Instead of copying the worksheet, you can move it. To do so, skip to step 6.

 Open the workbooks you want to copy from and copy to. Refer to Task 5 for more information on viewing multiple workbooks.

 Click the worksheet tab you want to copy (for example, **Regions 1 - 3**).

 Choose **Edit**, **Move or Copy Sheet** to open the Move or Copy dialog box.

 Click the **To Book** drop-down list and select the workbook you want to move it to (for example, **Book2**).

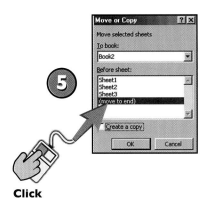

Click

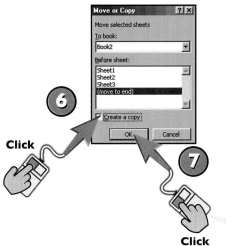

Click

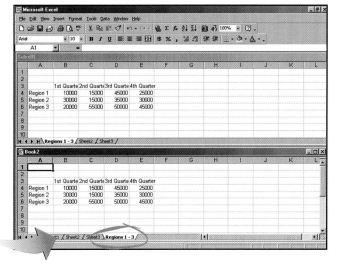

Click

Click

5. Select the tab order location you want to place the copy of the worksheet (for example, **(move to end)**).

6. Click the **Create a copy** check box.

7. Click the **OK** button. The worksheet is copied.

End Task

✓ **Copying to a New Workbook**
You can copy the worksheet to a new workbook by selecting (new book) from the **To Book** drop-down list.

Task 12: Zooming a Worksheet

Getting a Closer Look at Your Data

If you want to zoom in and get a closer look at data in your worksheet, you can select a higher percentage of magnification. On the other hand, if you want to zoom out so more of the worksheet shows on the screen at one glance, select a lower percentage of magnification.

Start Here

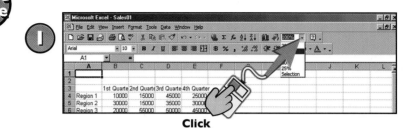

Click

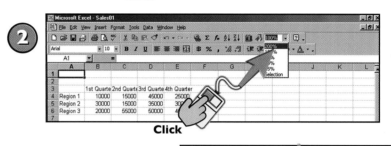

Click

✓ **Print Preview Zoom**
You also can zoom in Print Preview. Click on the worksheet to zoom in. Click again to zoom out. You also can click the **Zoom** button in the Print Preview toolbar.

✓ **Type the Percent**
Besides selecting one of the Zoom percentage options, you can click in the list box area and type the exact percentage.

1 Click the **Zoom** list box down arrow.

2 Click the zoom percentage you want. The worksheet appears in the selected view (for example, **200%**).

End Task

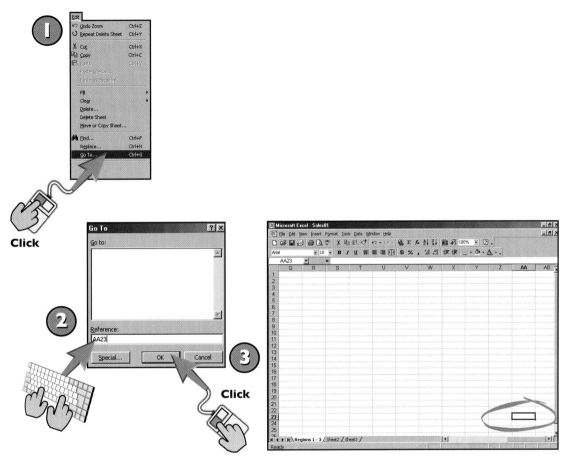

Click

Click

Using the Go To Command

Moving from cell to cell with the mouse or keyboard is fine when you want to move a short distance. If you want to move a farther distance, however, you might want to investigate the **Go To** command. This command enables you to move quickly to any cell in the worksheet.

1. Choose **Edit**, **Go To** to open the Go To dialog box.

2. Type the cell reference (for example, **AA23**).

3. Click the **OK** button. Excel moves to the selected cell.

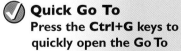

Quick Go To
Press the **Ctrl+G** keys to quickly open the Go To dialog box.

End
Task

Task 14: Freezing Rows and Columns

Creating a Non-Scrolling Region

Many times your worksheet will be so large that you cannot view all the data onscreen at the same time. In addition, if you have added row or column titles, and you scroll down or to the right, some of the titles will be too far to the top or left of the worksheet for you to see. For example, if you are reviewing data in column FF, it would be nice to see the row title of the cell you are referencing. To help, you can freeze the heading rows and columns so they're always visible.

✅ **Remove Frozen Panes**
To remove the freezing of columns and rows, choose **Window, Unfreeze Panes.**

✅ **Splitting a Worksheet**
If you want to split your worksheet to see multiple portions of your worksheet, see Task 15 "Splitting a Worksheet" for more information.

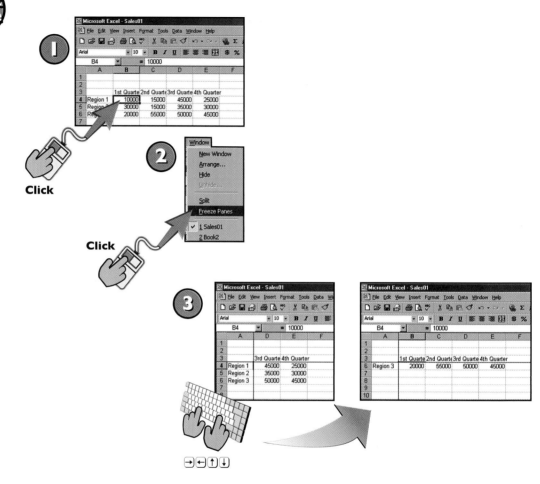

1. Click in the cell to the right and below the area you want to freeze (for example, **B4**).

2. Choose **Window, Freeze Panes**.

3. Move through the worksheet (use the arrow keys) and notice that the rows and columns you selected are frozen so you can reference data with the appropriate titles.

Task 15: Splitting a Worksheet

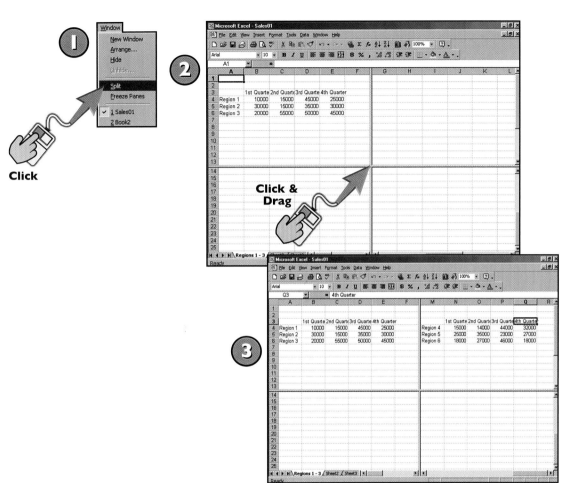

Click

Click & Drag

Separating a Worksheet

By splitting a worksheet you can scroll independently into different horizontal and vertical parts of a worksheet. This is useful if you want to view different parts of a worksheet or copy and paste between different areas of a large worksheet.

① Choose **Window**, **Split**.

② Click the horizontal and vertical split bars and drag them to the location you want for the horizontal split.

③ Move through the worksheet and see how easily you can view other parts of the worksheet simultaneously.

✓ **Return to a Single Pane**
Choose **Window, Remove Split** when you want to return to viewing your worksheet in one window.

✓ **Freezing Rows and Columns**
If you want to keep row and column labels visible as you work and scroll, see Task 14 "Freezing Rows and Columns" for more information.

End Task

PART 3

Editing Worksheets

The old paper and pencil method of calculating was a pain because if you made a mistake or forgot something, you had to do a lot or erasing—maybe even redo the whole thing. With an electronic worksheet, you can easily make changes. Forget something? You can insert a cell, row, or column. You also can delete entries. You can change a value, find and replace data, and even check for spelling errors. Besides editing the data in your worksheets, you can add comments to remind yourself of information and track who and when changes are made.

Tasks

Task 1: Editing Data

Altering Cell Data

If an entry is no longer valid—perhaps you entered the wrong number or the value changed—you can edit the entry. Being able to make changes to the values in your worksheet is what makes Excel such a valuable analysis tool. You can change any of your entries and see how that affects the formulas in your worksheet.

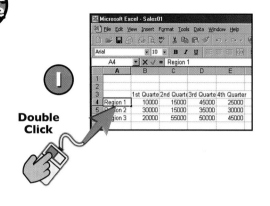

Double Click

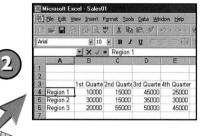

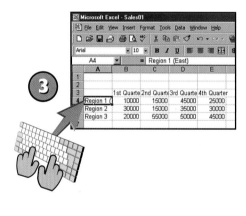

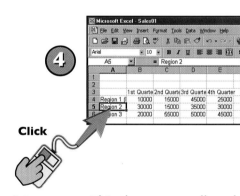

Click

✓ **Enter Key**
You can't press an arrow key to confirm the entry and move to another cell. You must press **Enter**.

1 Double-click the cell you want to edit. The insertion point appears within the current cell, and the entry also appears in the Formula Bar.

2 Press the left and right arrow keys to move the insertion point where you want to make the change.

3 Type in your changes (using the backspace key as necessary) and press the **Enter** key to accept your changes.

4 Click on another cell you would like to edit.

Next Step

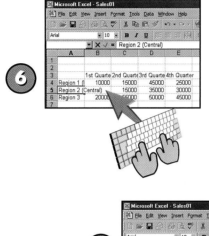

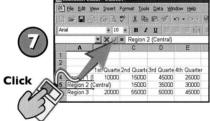

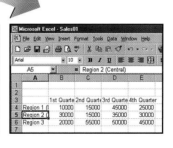

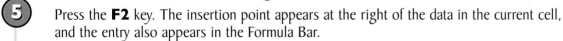

Click

Selecting Characters
You can drag the mouse pointer across characters to select them. Then press the **Delete** key to delete the selected characters.

(5) Press the **F2** key. The insertion point appears at the right of the data in the current cell, and the entry also appears in the Formula Bar.

(6) Type in your changes.

(7) Click the green check mark **Enter** button to accept the changes.

Copying and Moving
In addition to editing data, you might find it easier to copy and move the correct data to a different location. See Tasks 9 and 10 for more information on copying and moving data.

Task 2: Overwriting and Deleting Data

Getting Rid of Data

Overwriting a cell means replacing the cell's contents with new data. Overwriting is handy when you want to correct typing errors or when a cell contains the wrong data. You also can easily erase the contents of a cell by using the Delete key. Erasing a cell is useful when you change your mind about the contents after you enter the data in the cell. Sometimes you might find that data you initially typed into a cell is incorrect and needs to be changed.

⊘ WARNING

Be careful not to overwrite formulas if that is not what you intended. If you overwrite a formula with a constant value, Excel no longer updates the formula. If you accidentally overwrite a formula but you've saved your spreadsheet recently, you can reopen the spreadsheet to a version saved before you overwrote the formula.

Start Here

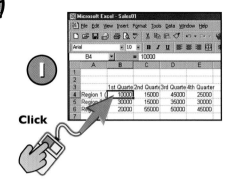

Click

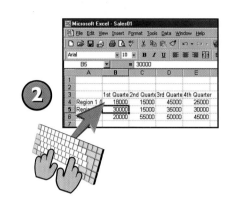

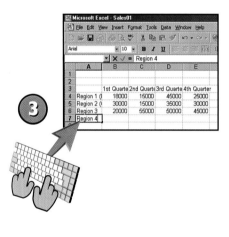

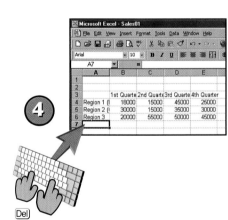

Del

① Click on the cell you want to overwrite, making it the active cell (for example, **B4**).

② Type the correct data into the cell (for example, **18000**) and press the **Enter** key.

③ Type additional text in you worksheet (for example, **Region 4** in cell **A7**) and make it the active cell.

④ Press the **Delete** key on the keyboard to delete the data you just added.

End Task

Task 3: Undoing and Redoing Changes

Start Here

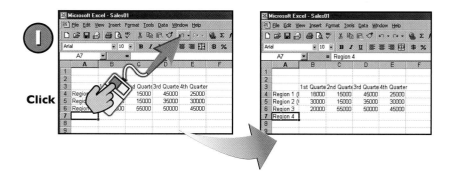

Click

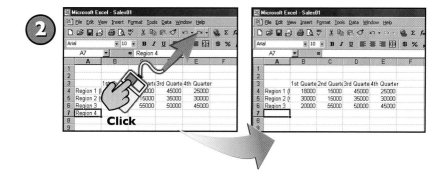

Click

Using Undo and Redo

Many times you will find you are making numerous changes to your worksheets and need to undo some of the changes. Excel enables you to undo changes and redo them so you can quickly see the differences between the two.

✓ **Multiple Undo and Redo**
Instead of using the drop-down arrows, you can click the Undo and Redo buttons as many times as necessary to get your worksheet back to the way you want it.

✓ **Keyboard Undo**
A quick and easy way to undo an action is to simultaneously press the **Ctrl+Z** keys on the keyboard.

① Click the **Undo** button on the Standard toolbar to undo each change you recently made.

② Click the **Redo** button on the Standard toolbar to redo each change you recently made.

End Task

Task 4: Inserting Cells

Adding Cells

There might be times when you entered data into your worksheet and noticed that you typed the wrong information, so you are off by one cell in a column or row. To avoid retyping all the data, you can insert cells and shift the current cells to their correct locations.

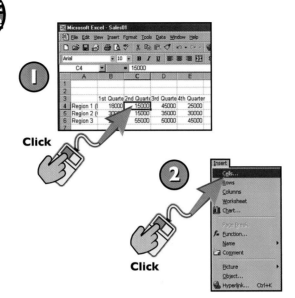

Start Here

Click

Click

✅ **Using the Shortcut Menu**
Another way to insert a cell is to right-click on a cell and choose **Insert** from the shortcut menu to open the Insert dialog box.

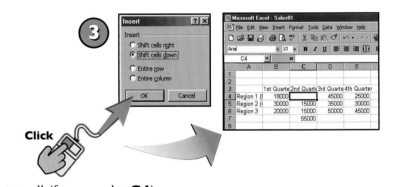

Click

① Select where you want to insert a cell (for example, **C4**).

② Choose **Insert**, **Cells** to open the Insert dialog box.

③ Click the **OK** button to accept the **Shift Cells Down** default option when you insert the cells. Everything below cell C4 is shifted down a cell.

End Task

Task 5: Deleting Cells

Start Here

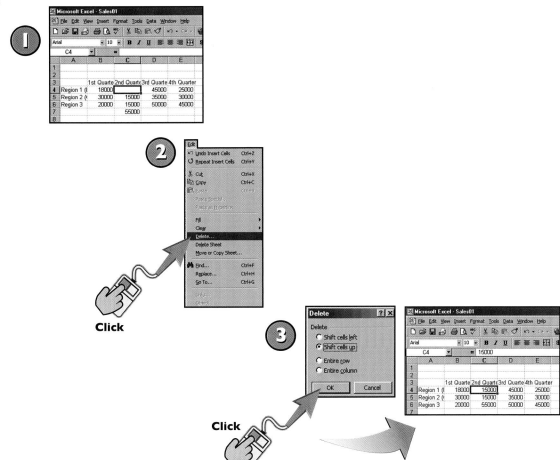

Click

Click

Removing Cells

Sometimes when you're working with worksheets, you will find that data needs to be eliminated to keep the worksheet up to date. Or, perhaps you added an extraneous cell of data in a row or column. To avoid retyping all the data again, you can delete cells and shift the current cells to their correct locations.

✓ **#REF! Error**
If the #REF! error appears in a cell after you make a deletion, it means you deleted data your worksheet needs to calculate a formula. Undo the change; Task 3 tells you how. For more on formulas, see Part 5, "Working with Formulas and Functions."

I Select the cells you want to delete (for example, cell **C4**).

2 Choose **Edit**, **Delete** to open the Delete dialog box.

3 Click the **OK** button to accept the **Shift Cells Up** default option when you delete the cells. Everything below cell C4 is shifted up a cell.

End Task

Task 6: Inserting Rows and Columns

Adding Rows and Columns

You can insert extra rows to make more room for additional data or formulas. Adding more rows, which gives the appearance of adding space between rows, can also make the worksheet easier to read. You can insert extra columns to make room for more data or formulas. Adding more space between columns also makes the worksheet easier to read.

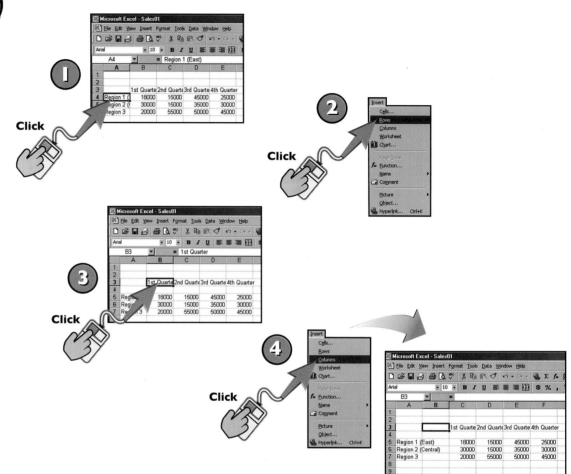

Start Here

Click

Click

Click

Click

✓ Automatic Formula Row Updates

When you insert a new row or column, Excel automatically updates any formulas affected by the insertion (see Part 5, "Working with Formulas and Functions," for more information).

1 Click the cell you want to add a row above (for example, **A4**).

2 Choose **Insert**, **Rows** to insert a row below the column titles.

3 Click the cell you want to add a column to the left of (for example, **B3**).

4 Choose **Insert**, **Columns** to insert a column to the left of the row titles.

End Task

Task 7: Deleting Rows and Columns

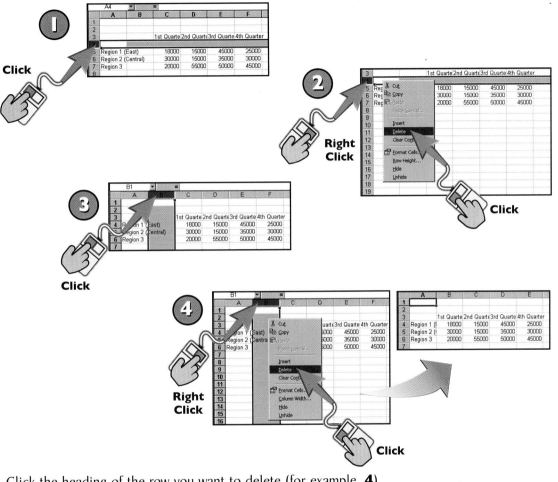

Click

Right Click

Click

Click

Right Click

Click

Removing Rows and Columns

You can delete rows from a worksheet to close up some empty space or remove unwanted information. You might want to delete columns from a worksheet to close up some empty space or remove unwanted information.

✓ #REF! Error
If the #REF! error appears in a cell after you delete a row, it means you deleted a cell or cells that contained data your worksheet needs to calculate a formula. Undo the change; Task 3 tells you how.

---

① Click the heading of the row you want to delete (for example, **4**).

② Right-click and choose **Delete** from the shortcut menu.

③ Click the column heading of the column you want to delete (for example, **B**).

④ Right-click and choose **Delete** from the shortcut menu.

End Task

Task 8: Flipping Rows and Columns

Transposing a Worksheet

Transposing (flipping rows and columns) is a special copy feature you might need to use if you want to change the layout of your worksheet. Suppose that your worksheet is set up with quarters in rows and divisions in columns. Your boss prefers the opposite: quarters in columns and divisions in rows. You can flip-flop the worksheet.

Click

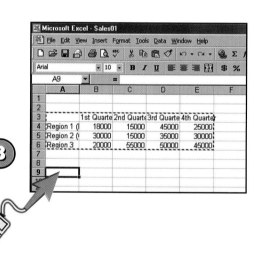

Click

1 Select the range you want to transpose.

2 Click the **Copy** button.

3 Click the first cell in which you want to paste the range.

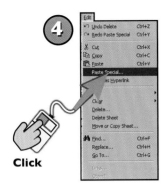

Click

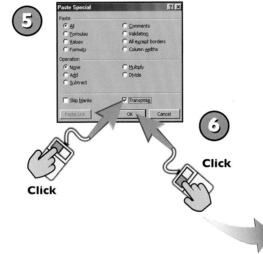

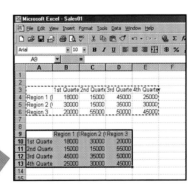

Click

Click

Click

✓ **Paste Special**
Notice that the Paste Special dialog box enables you to paste all different types of formulas, values, formats, and so on. Practice using this dialog box and see the different types of results that you get.

✓ **Original Data**
To eliminate the original data that you transposed, you must delete it. See Task 2 "Overwriting and Deleting Data" for more information.

④ Choose **Edit**, **Paste Special**. You see the Paste Special dialog box.

⑤ Click the **Transpose** check box.

⑥ Click the **OK** button. The range is transposed (or flipped).

Task 9: Cutting, Copying, and Pasting Data

Reusing Information

You can save the time and trouble of retyping information in the worksheet by copying cells and pasting them over and over again. A great new feature in Office 2000 is the capability to cut, copy, and paste as many as 12 different items at a time. For example, if you need to copy two different selections of data from the beginning of a worksheet to two different locations toward the end of a worksheet, you can do the procedure in fewer steps with the *Clipboard* than if you copy and paste each separately.

✓ **Cut Versus Copy**
When you want to move data from its current location and place it in a new location (rather than copying it), click the **Cut** button on the Standard toolbar instead of the **Copy** button. The Cut option actually removes the selected value from the old location.

Start Here

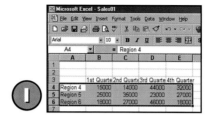

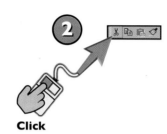

Click

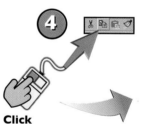

Click

① Select the cells that you want to *cut* and paste.

② Click the **Cut** button on the Standard toolbar.

③ Select the cells that you want to *copy* and paste.

④ Click the **Copy** button on the Standard toolbar again. Notice that the Clipboard window appears.

Next Step

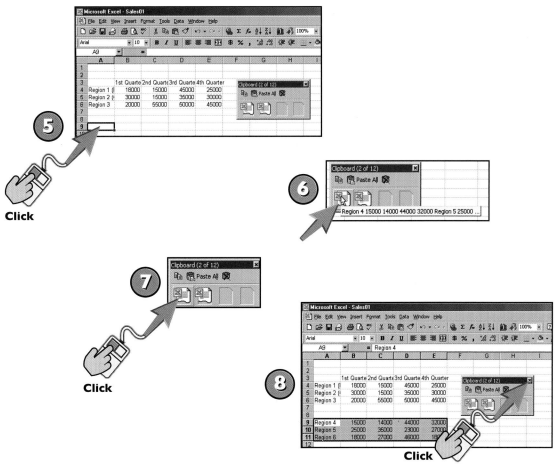

Using the Clipboard

If you want to clear all the items copied to the Clipboard, click the **Clear Clipboard** button. If you want to copy all the items saved to the Clipboard in one location, click the **Paste All** button. If you don't want to use the Clipboard window, click the **Close** button when it appears.

Keeping the Clipboard Open

You can keep the Clipboard window open and use the buttons while you work. It might be easier to move the Clipboard window out of the way by dragging and dropping it like a toolbar or docking it with your other toolbars (see Part 1, Task 7 "Working with Toolbars," for more information).

Pasting Formulas

If you paste cells using Ctrl+V you can paste cell *formulas*. If you paste cells with formulas from the multi-element Clipboard, you paste the *values*, not the formulas.

Click

Click

5 Click to place the cursor in the worksheet where you want to paste the data.

6 Move the mouse pointer over the Clipboard items and a ScreenTip displays what is contained in each copied clip.

7 Click the **Clip** button on the Clipboard window of the item you want to paste.

8 Click the **Close (X)** button to return to the worksheet.

Task 10: Moving Data

Putting Data Somewhere Else

Excel lets you move information from one cell and place it into another cell. You do not have to go to the new cell and enter the same data and then erase the data in the old location. For example, you might want to move data in a worksheet because the layout of the worksheet has changed.

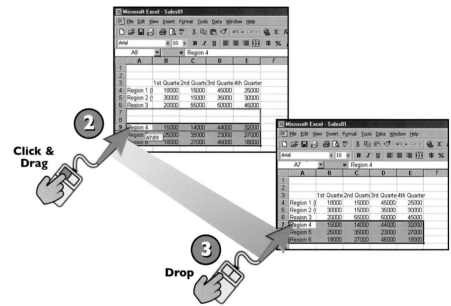

Click & Drag

Drop

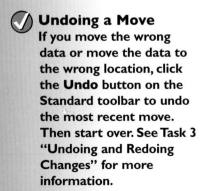

✓ **Undoing a Move**
If you move the wrong data or move the data to the wrong location, click the **Undo** button on the Standard toolbar to undo the most recent move. Then start over. See Task 3 "Undoing and Redoing Changes" for more information.

1 Select the cells you want to move (for example, **A9:E11**).

2 Click on the border of the selected cells and drag the cells to the location where you want to paste the cell data (for example, **A7:E9**).

3 Drop the data you are moving and it remains in the new location.

Task 11: Finding Data

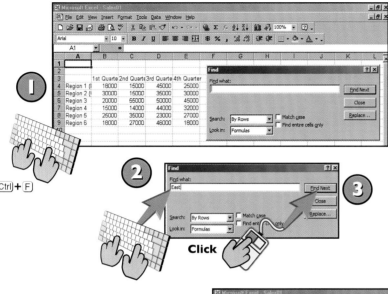

Ctrl + F

Click

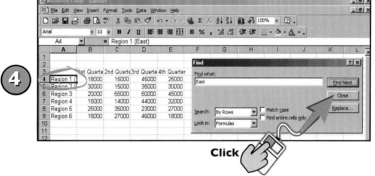

Click

Using Find

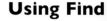

You'll sometimes need to find specific information in a large spreadsheet. For example, suppose you want to quickly find the row that deals with sales data in a particular region. This worksheet is small, so it's not hard to find the information, but it serves as a simple example.

1 Press **Ctrl+F** to open the Find dialog box.

2 Type the data you would like to find (for example, **East**) in the **Find What** text box.

3 Choose **Find Next**. Excel immediately finds the first instance of the information (if it exists in the worksheet) and makes it the active cell.

4 Click the **Close** button to end the search.

✓ **Finding Other Instances of Data**
Another way to search for data is to choose **Edit, Find**. To continue searching for more occurrences of a Find criterion, click the **Find Next** button.

End Task

Task 12: Replacing Data

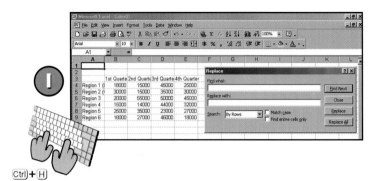

Using Find and Replace

It might happen that you are working in a workbook and you notice you need to alter multiple cells of data. Perhaps you spelled a company name incorrectly throughout the workbook, or maybe you just want to enhance the data (for example, capitalizing a particular word throughout).

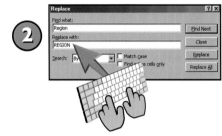

Ctrl + H

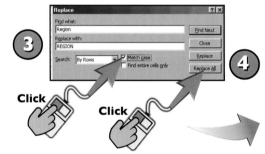

Click   Click

 Press **Ctrl+H** on the keyboard to open the Replace dialog box.

 Type the data you would like to find in the **Find What** text box, press the Tab key, and type the data you would like to replace it with in the **Replace With** text box.

 Click the **Match Case** check box so it contains a check mark. With this box checked, "region" doesn't match "REGION". With this box unchecked, "region" matches "REGION".

 Click the **Replace All** button; Excel makes the changes and closes the Replace dialog box.

Task 13: Adding Cell Comments

Start Here

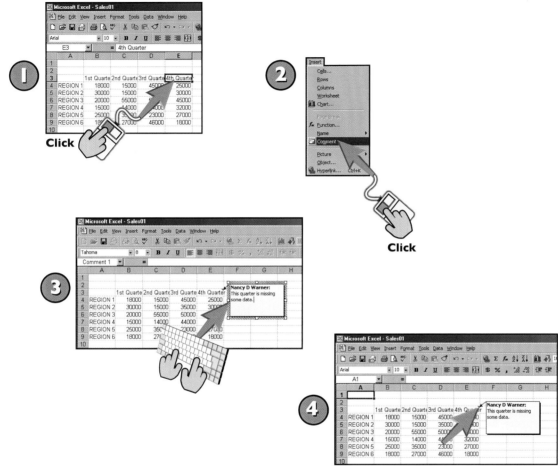

Click

Click

Adding Notes to a Cell

Some cells contain data or formulas that require an explanation or special attention. Comments provide a way to attach this type of information to individual cells without cluttering the cells with extraneous information. A red triangle indicates that a cell contains a comment, which you can view in several different ways.

1. Click the cell to which you want to add a comment (for example, **E3**).

2. Choose **Insert**, **Comment**.

3. Type the text into the comment area and click in the worksheet area to accept the comment. Notice that the cell's upper-right corner is now red to indicate the comment.

4. Move the mouse pointer over the comment marker in the cell to view the comment in a ScreenTip.

✔ Working with Comments

You can quickly add, edit, or delete a comment by right-clicking the mouse on the cell that contains the comment marker and selecting the correct command from the shortcut menu. Also see Task 14 "Editing and Deleting Cell Comments" for more information.

End Task

Altering Notes in a Cell

You can quickly edit or delete a comment by right-clicking the mouse on the cell that contains the comment marker and selecting either **Edit Comment** or **Delete Comment** from the shortcut menu.

✓ **Show Comments**
You can make it so that Excel displays the full text of a cell's comments while you are working in the worksheet. Right-click the commented cell and choose **Show Comment**. The comment then displays. If you want to hide the comment later, right-click the commented cell and choose **Hide Comment**.

Task 14: Editing and Deleting Cell Comments

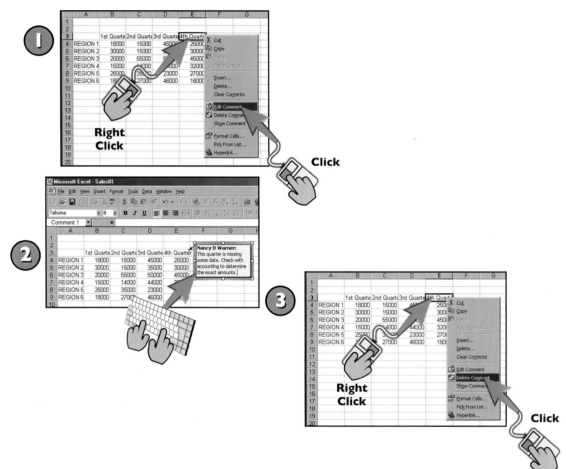

Right Click

Click

Right Click

Click

1   Right-click the cell to which you want to edit a comment and choose **Edit Comment** from the shortcut menu.

2   Type the edits into the comment area and click in the worksheet area to accept the comment.

3   Right-click the cell to which you want to edit a comment and choose **Delete Comment** from the shortcut menu.

End Task

Task 15: Protecting and Sharing Workbooks

Start Here

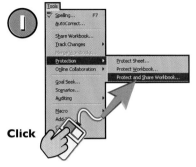

Click

Click

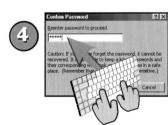

Assigning File Sharing Options

When you share files with other users, you might find it useful to protect your workbooks. You can protect your workbooks by restricting access to the workbook and preventing changes being made within each particular workbook. The three protection options are: protect sheet, protect workbook, and protect and share workbook. (To unprotect your workbook after you protected it, choose **Tools, Protection, Unprotect Shared Workbook**.)

⚠ WARNING

Don't forget the password you assign to your workbooks, if you forget or misplace the password, you will not be able to access the workbook. Choose a password you can remember but that others can't guess. Avoid names of pets or family.

① Choose **Tools**, **Protection**, **Protect and Share Workbook** to open the Protect Shared Workbook dialog box. This sets tracking changes so they cannot be turned off (see next task).

② Click the **Sharing with track changes** option (this activates the optional password text box) and then press the **Tab** key.

③ Type a password in the **Password (optional)** option and press the **Enter** key. This means that any other user will need to enter this password to open this workbook.

④ Type the same password in the Confirm Password dialog box and press the **Enter** key. (If asked to save the workbook, choose **OK**.)

End Task

Task 16: Tracking Changes

Keeping Track of Revision Marks

Excel lets you track changes that have been made to your worksheets. This is convenient when you are working on a team project in which multiple people are writing a report. For example, each person who adds data to the workbook can turn revision marks on so any changes they make show up in a different color from changes other team members make. The only time the colors won't be different is when two people use the same computer or user information (login or password).

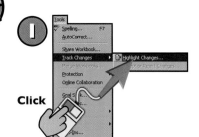

Start Here

Click

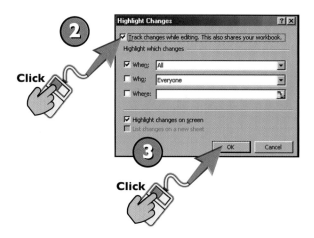

Click

Click

✓ **Shared Workbooks**
If you performed the tasks in Task 20, the option in step 2 will not be available. This is because you will automatically be tracking changes if your workbook is shared.

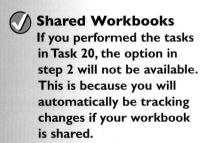

1 Choose **Tools**, **Track Changes**, **Highlight Changes** to open the Highlight Changes dialog box.

2 Click the **Track changes while editing**. This also shares your workbook option. If this isn't an option, see the "Shared Workbooks" tip.

3 Click the **OK** button. A message box appears telling you this action will save the workbook and asking if you want to continue.

Next Step

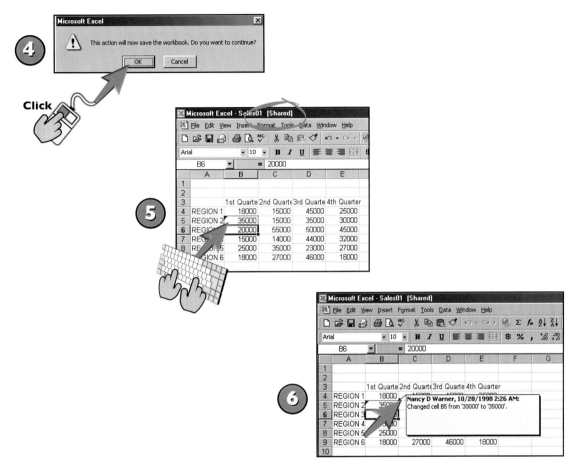

Tracked Changes

Excel remembers the previous value for a tracked change in case you want to go back; Task 25 explains how.

Shared Workbooks

Notice the word [Shared] in the title bar. This means that other people can use the workbook. This is useful in a network setting, where others can easily access your worksheet via the network. When you turn tracking marks on, you automatically share the workbook. In the Highlight dialog box, deselect the check box next to **Track changes while editing**. This also shares your workbook. This turns track marks off and stops sharing your workbook.

4 Click the **OK** button and the workbook title bar states that the workbook is **[Shared]**.

5 Type a change in a cell (for example, cell **B5**) and press the **Enter** key. Notice the cell now has a comment marker in the upper-left corner and colored border.

6 Move the mouse pointer over the revised cell and a ScreenTip appears, showing the change that was made and who made the change.

Task 17: Accepting or Rejecting Tracked Changes

Keeping or Discarding Revision Marks

When you are ready to finalize any tracked changes that have been made to a worksheet, you need to determine which changes you want to accept or reject. If you accept a change, Excel keeps it. If you reject a change, Excel restores the previous value and deletes the tracked change.

✓ Accepting and Rejecting

In the Select Changes to Accept or Reject dialog box, click the **Reject** button to return the tracked mark back to the original text; click the **Accept** button to accept a tracked change as you review the workbook changes; or click the **Reject All** button to reject all changes that have been made to the workbook.

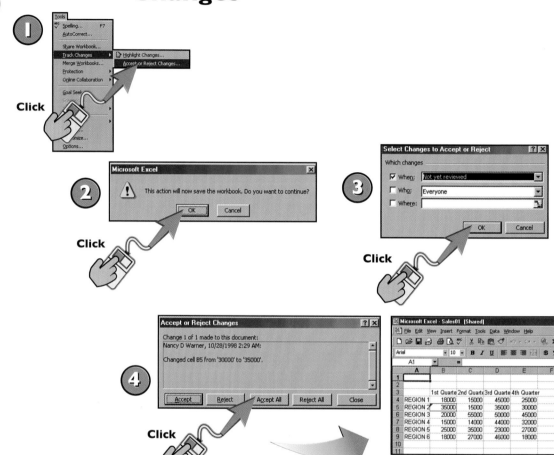

Choose **Tools**, **Track Changes**, **Accept or Reject Changes**.

Click the **OK** button in the message box that appears telling you this action will save the workbook, unless you just recently saved the workbook.

Click the **OK** button to accept the default options in the list boxes for **When**, **Who**, and **Where** you want to accept or reject a change.

Click the **Accept All** button to accept all changes in the workbook. Notice that the comment marker remains for your reference.

Task 18: Checking Spelling

Start Here

Click

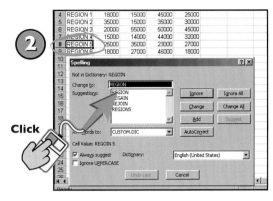

Click

Click

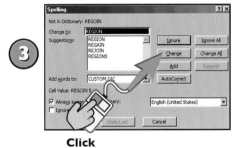

Click

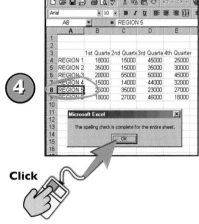

Click

Making Sure Your Data Is Spelled Correctly

Many people take spelling in workbooks for granted. But, if you turn in a report to your manager, he might not like seeing spelling errors and mistakes. You can check spelling in Excel 2000 quickly and easily. Of course, you should always review your workbooks, but it never hurts to have a little help.

✓ Check from the Beginning

You don't have to be at the beginning of a workbook when you check for spelling errors. If you start in the middle of a workbook, Excel checks until it reaches the end and then asks you whether you want to continue checking from the beginning of your workbook.

---

1 Click the **Spelling** button on the Standard toolbar. The Spelling and Grammar dialog box opens, displaying the first spelling or grammar error it finds.

2 Click the appropriate spelling option in the **Suggestions** list box (for example, **REGION**).

3 Click the **Change** button. Excel makes the change in the workbook and moves to the next error it finds.

4 Click the **OK** button when Excel displays a message telling you the spelling check is complete. This means all inaccuracies have been reviewed.

End Task

4

Formatting Worksheet Data

Formatting a worksheet means you can change the appearance of the data on it. With Excel's formatting tools, you can make your worksheet more attractive and readable. Numeric values are usually more than just numbers—they can represent a dollar value, a date, a percent, or some other value.

Tasks

Task 1: Applying Styles to Numeric Data

Working with Styles

You can apply different styles to cells, depending on the type of data the cells contain. Using styles affects the way cells display data but does not limit the type of data you can enter. By placing data into a style, you can display it in a familiar format that makes it easier to read. For example, sales numbers are usually styled in a currency format.

✓ **Choose Other Styles**
Numerous other styles are available for applying to data. For a wider selection, select **Format, Cells** and click through the many **Category** options.

✓ **Currency Style**
When you select the Currency Style button, your numbers are automatically formatted with a dollar sign ($), commas, and a decimal point out to two places. In addition, the column size increases automatically to fit the width of the newly styled data.

Start Here

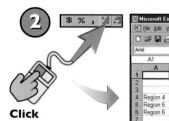

Click

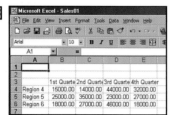

Click

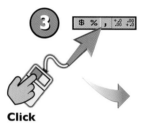

Click

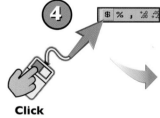

Click

1 Select the cells you want to format.

2 Click twice on the **Increase Decimal** button on the Formatting toolbar.

3 Click the **Comma Style** button on the Formatting toolbar.

4 Click the **Currency Style** button on the Formatting toolbar.

End Task

Task 2: Using a General Format

Start Here

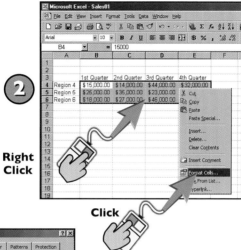

Right Click

Click

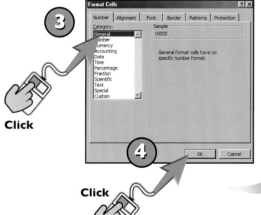

Click

Click

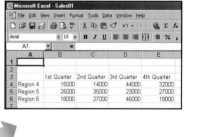

End Task

Displaying No Specific Format

When you enter numbers into Excel cells, the default format is General. The cells will not have a specific number format. For example, this is used when you are recording counts of items, incrementing numbers, or do not require any particular format.

✓ **Quick General Format**
Another way to quickly format numbers in the general format that you have altered is to choose **Edit, Clear, Formats.** Excel clears all the formatting and returns the numbers to their original general format (unless you originally entered them in a different format).

1. Select the cells you want to format.

2. Right-click the selected cells and choose **Format Cells** from the Shortcut menu.

3. Click the **Category** option of **General** on the Number tab of the Format Cells dialog box.

4. Click the **OK** button. Excel changes the format.

Task 3: Using a Number Format

Displaying Numbers

The Number format in Excel defaults to two decimal places. You have the option to alter the number of decimal places, use a comma separator, and even determine the way you want negative numbers to appear (for example, a minus sign, in red, in parentheses, or a combination).

✓ **Fraction Format**
This format enables you to determine the type of fraction you want to appear and the number of digits that are displayed. In addition, you can set your numbers to default to common halves, quarters, and so on.

✓ **Scientific Format**
This format enables you to assign decimal places. The default scientific format is two decimal places, for example, 88000.26.

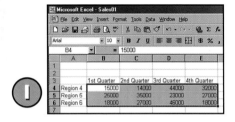

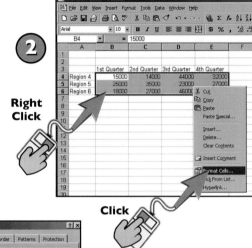

Right Click

Click

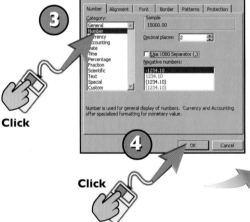

Click

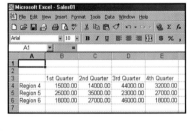

Click

1 Select the cells you want to format.

2 Right-click the selected cells and choose **Format Cells** from the Shortcut menu.

3 Click the **Category** option of **Number** on the Number tab of the Format Cells dialog box.

4 Click the **OK** button. Excel changes the format.

Task 4: Using a Currency Format

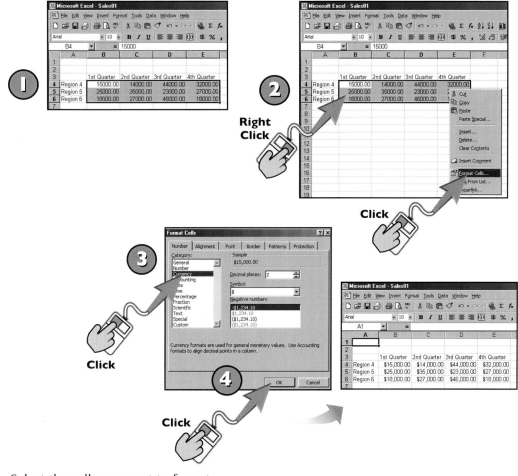

Right Click

Click

Click

Click

Click

Displaying Monetary Values

The Currency format in Excel defaults to two decimal places. You do have the option to alter the number of decimal places, display a dollar sign, and even determine the way you want negative numbers to appear (for example, a minus sign, in red, in parentheses, or a combination).

✓ **Accounting Format**
This format automatically lines up the currency symbols and decimal points for the cells in a column.

✓ **Percentage Format**
This format multiplies the cell value by 100 and displays the result with a percent symbol. You need to be careful when entering percentages to make sure you don't get inaccurate results. For example, if you want to display 25%, you need to have .25 entered in the cell, otherwise it appears as 2500%.

---

① Select the cells you want to format.

② Right-click the selected cells and choose **Format Cells** from the Shortcut menu.

③ Click the **Category** option of **Currency** on the **Number** tab of the Format Cells dialog box.

④ Click the **OK** button. Excel changes the format.

Task 5: Using a Date Format

Displaying Date Serial Numbers

The Date format in Excel displays the date and time serial numbers as date values. There are numerous different date types you can assign to your dates. For example, you might find it easier to skim through dates as numbers with or without the assigned year visible. Or, perhaps you would rather use the actual name of the month for reference.

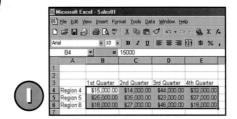

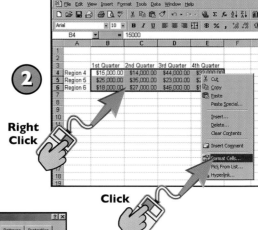

Right Click

Click

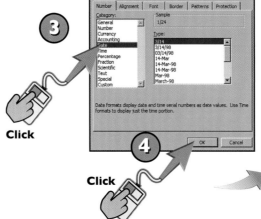

Click

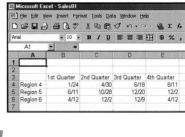

Click

✓ **Time and Custom Formats**

You can use the Time format if you want to display just the time portion. In addition, you can use the Custom format option to create a Date and Time format.

 Select the cells you want to format.

 Right-click the selected cells and choose **Format Cells** from the Shortcut menu.

 Click the **Category** option of **Date** on the Number tab of the Format Cells dialog box.

 Click the **OK** button. Excel changes the format.

End Task

Task 6: Using a Text Format

Start Here

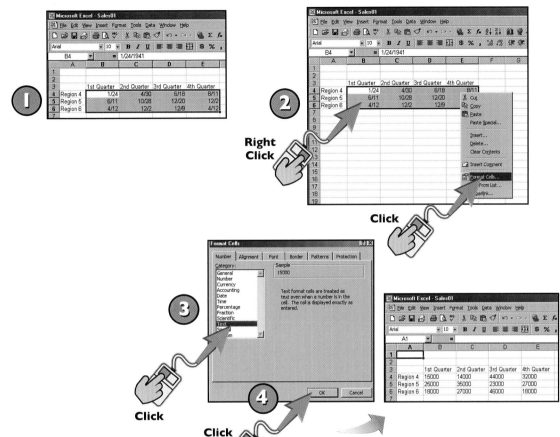

Right Click

Click

Click

Click

Displaying a Number as Text

The Text format displays numbers as text no matter if the data in the cell is a number or text. This can be convenient if you want to enter a number but want to make sure it is never used in any type of formula or function.

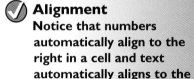

✓ **Alignment**
Notice that numbers automatically align to the right in a cell and text automatically aligns to the left in a cell.

✓ **Immediate Number Text**
Another way to immediately make a number a textual cell entry is to type an apostrophe (') before you type in the number, this tells Excel that the number is to be text.

1 Select the cells you want to format.

2 Right-click the selected cells and choose **Format Cells** from the Shortcut menu.

3 Click the **Category** option of **Text** on the Number tab of the Format Cells dialog box.

4 Click the **OK** button. Excel changes the format.

End Task

Task 7: Applying Bold, Italic, and Underline

Formatting Data

You can format the data contained in one or more cells to draw attention to it or make it easier to find. Numbers attract attention when formatted with bold, italic, or underline. Indicating summary values, questionable data, or any other cells, is easy with formatting.

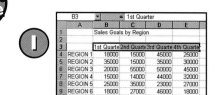

Click

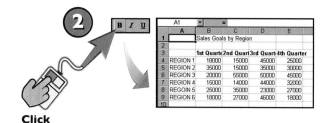

Click

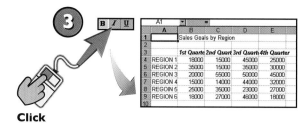

Click

✓ **Combination Formatting**

You can use several formatting techniques in combination, such as bold and italic or italic and underline.

(1) Select the cells you want to format.

(2) Click the **Bold** button on the Formatting toolbar.

(3) Click the **Italic** button on the Formatting toolbar.

(4) Click the **Underline** button on the Formatting toolbar.

End Task

Task 8: Changing Alignment

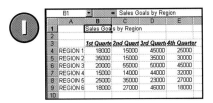

Click

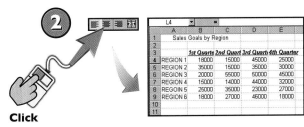

Click

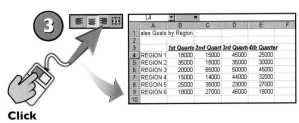

Click

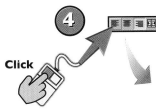

Aligning Data in a Cell

Excel provides several ways to format data. One way is to align data. The most common alignment changes you make will probably be to center data in a cell, align data with a cell's right edge (right-aligned), or align data with a cell's left edge (left-aligned). The default alignment for numbers is right-aligned; the default alignment for text is left-aligned.

① Select the cells you want to align.

② Click the **Center** button on the Formatting toolbar.

③ Click the **Align Right** button on the Formatting toolbar.

④ Click the **Align Left** button on the Formatting toolbar.

 Default Alignment
After you select text to align, if you click the same alignment button a second time, the cell returns to its default alignment.

Page **71**

Task 9: Wrapping Text in a Cell

Using the Wrap Text Feature

Excel provides several ways to format data. One way is to allow text to wrap in a cell. Many times a heading (row or column, for example) is longer than the width of the cell holding the data. If you are trying to make your worksheet organized and readable, wrap text so it is completely visible in a cell.

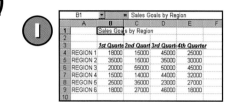

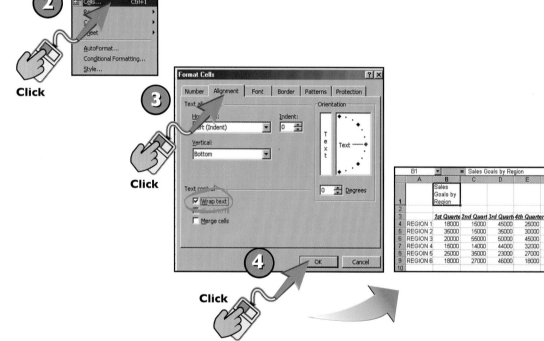

Start Here

Click

Click

Click

✓ **Align Wrapped Text**
You can align text that has been wrapped. Sometimes this gives a cleaner look to your text. See Task 8 to learn how to align text in a cell.

1 Select the cells that you want to wrap text.

2 Choose **Format**, **Cells** to open the Format Cells dialog box.

3 Click the **Alignment** tab and select **Wrap Text** in the Text Control area.

4 Click the **OK** button.

End Task

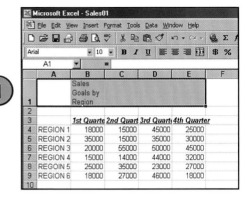

Task 10: Using Merge and Center on a Cell

Click

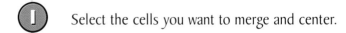

Merging Cells

Excel provides several ways to format data. One way is to use the **Merge and Center** feature. Columns of data usually have column headers, but they can also have group header information within a set of columns. For example, you might have four quarters' worth of sales data for the past two years, but want to have a header that distinguishes each set of quarters by their year.

① Select the cells you want to merge and center.

② Click the **Merge and Center** button on the Formatting toolbar.

✅ Undoing Merged and Centered Cells

You undo a set of merged and centered cells by first selecting the set of cells that are merged together. Choose **Format, Cells.** Then click the **Alignment** tab and click the **Merge Cells** check box to deselect this option.

Task 11: Changing Borders

Working with Cell Borders

Each side of a cell is considered a border. These borders provide a visual cue as to where a cell begins and ends. You can customize borders to indicate other beginnings and endings, such as grouping similar data or separating headings from data. For example, a double line is often used to separate a summary value from the data being totaled. Changing the bottom of the border for the last number before the total accomplishes this effect.

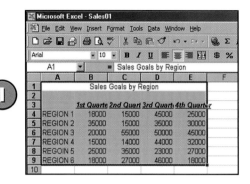

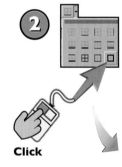

Click

✓ Removing Borders
To remove a border, click the **No Border** option from the Borders drop-down menu.

✓ Floating Toolbar
You can click the top of the Borders drop-down menu and drag the menu to make it a floating toolbar.

 Select the cells to which you want add some type of border.

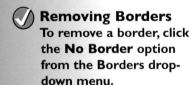 Click the border option (for example, **Thick Box Border**) on the **Borders** drop-down menu.

End Task

Task 12: Choosing Font Settings

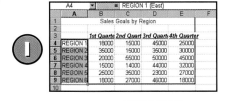

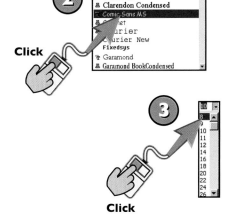

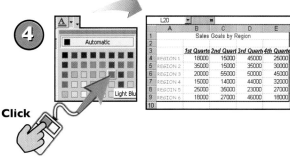

Click

Click

Click

Changing Typefaces

You can format data by changing the font used to display it. Changing the font gives data a different look and feel, which can help differentiate the type of data a cell contains. You can also change the font's size and color for added emphasis. For example, you can display different columns of data in different colors to differentiate them.

✓ Fonts Sample

New in Office 2000 is the capability to see a sample of a font in the Font drop-down list box. You can see what the font looks like before you apply it to your cells. This helps you choose the right font faster.

✓ Format Options

To format only a portion of a cell's data, select only that portion and then change the font. You can also select a font color (or other options) before you begin typing. Then all of the data in a cell will be that color.

---

1 Select the cells you want to format.

2 Click the **Font** drop-down list and choose the font you would like to apply to the cells (for example, **Comic Sans MS**).

3 Click the **Font Size** drop-down list and choose the font size you would like to apply to the cells (for example, **8**).

4 Click the **Font Color** drop-down menu and choose the font color you would like to apply to the cell (for example, **Light Blue**).

Coloring Cells

Generally, cells present a white background for displaying data. However, you can apply other colors or shading to the background. In addition, you can combine these colors with various patterns for a more attractive effect. As with most formatting options, this can help emphasize more important data.

⚠ WARNING

Be sure a shading or color pattern doesn't interfere with the readability of the data. The data still needs to be clear; you might need to make the text bold or choose a complementary text color. If you're going to print the worksheet to a non-color printer, the color you choose will print gray. The darker the gray, the less readable the data. Yellow generally prints to a pleasing light gray that doesn't compete with the data.

Task 13: Filling Cell Color

Click

1   Select the cells you want to color.

2   Click the shading or color you would like to apply on the **Fill Color** drop-down menu (for example, **Gray-25%**).

Task 14: Changing Cell Orientation

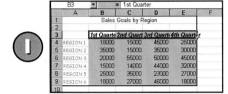

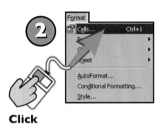

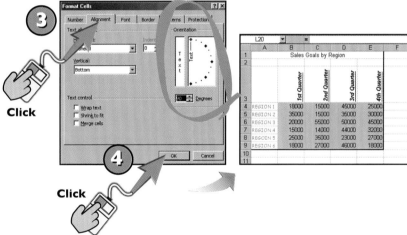

Click

Click

Click

Excel lets you alter the orientation of cells—that is, the angle at which it displays information. The main reason for doing this is to help draw attention to important or special text. This feature can be convenient when you have a lot of columns in a worksheet and you don't want your column headers to take up much horizontal space, or you just want the information to stand out.

1. Select the cells that you want to alter the orientation.

2. Choose **Format**, **Cells** to open the Format Cells dialog box.

3. Click the **Alignment** tab and try the orientation options in the Orientation area (for example, **90 Degrees**).

4. Click the **OK** button.

 Rotating Data
In the Orientation section of the Alignment dialog box, click on the half circle to change the angle at which data is rotated within the selected cell(s).

Task 15: Changing Row Height

Sizing Rows

Depending on the other formatting changes you make to a cell, data might not display properly. Increasing the font size or forcing data to wrap around within a cell might prevent data from being entirely displayed or cause it to run over into other cells. You can frequently avoid these problems by resizing rows.

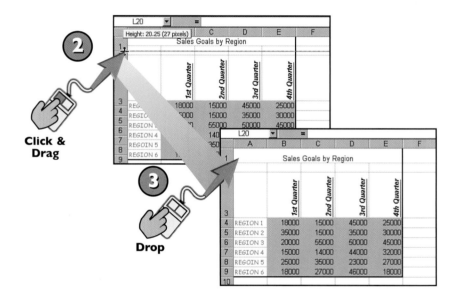

Start Here

Click & Drag

Drop

✓ **Multiple Rows, Same Height**

To make multiple rows the same height, click the mouse and drag over all the row headers you want resized. Then resize one of the rows. Each row becomes that size.

✓ **AutoFit Rows**

To automatically make a row fit the height of the tallest cell, choose **Format, Row, AutoFit**.

1 Move the mouse pointer over the bottom edge of the row header you want to alter. The pointer changes to a two-headed arrow.

2 Click and drag the row edge to the new size.

3 Release the mouse button to drop the line in the new location.

End Task

Task 16: Changing Column Width

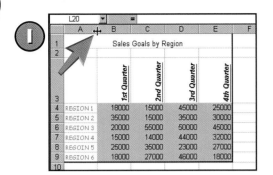

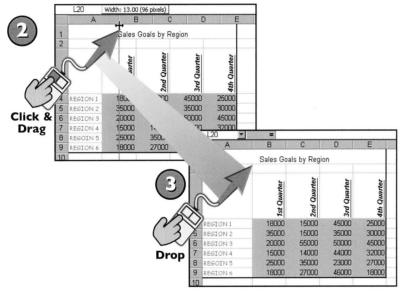

Click & Drag

Drop

Resizing Columns

Many times, data is too wide to be displayed within a cell. Excel provides several alternatives for remedying this problem. You can select columns and either specify a width or force Excel to automatically adjust the width of a cell to exactly fit its contents.

---

1 Move the mouse pointer over the side of the column header you want to alter (the pointer changes to a two-headed arrow).

2 Click and drag the column edge to the new size.

3 Release the mouse button to drop the line in the new location.

✓ **Multiple Columns, Same Width**
To make multiple columns the same width, click the mouse and drag over all the column headers you want resized. Then resize one of the columns. Each column becomes that size.

✓ **AutoFit Columns**
To automatically make a column fit the width of the widest cell, choose **Format, Column, AutoFit Selection.**

Aligning Subcategories

Another alignment you might want to use is to indent entries within a cell. Doing so can show the organization of entries; for example, subcategories of a budget category.

Task 17: Indenting Entries in a Cell

Click

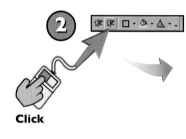

Click

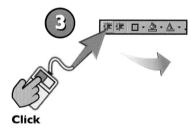

✓ **Increase Column Width**

To make the effect of the indent stand out, you might need to increase the width of the indented column. To do so, see Task 16 "Changing Column Width."

 Select the cell or range you want to indent.

 Click the **Increase Indent** button the number of times you want the entries indented.

 Click the **Decrease Indent** button to decrease the number of indents.

End Task

Task 18: Hiding Rows and Columns

Start Here

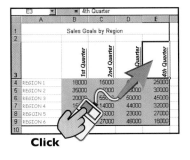

Click

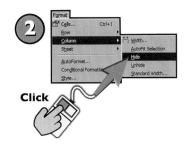

Click

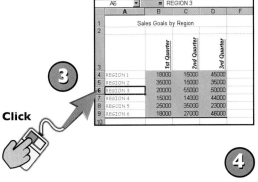

Click

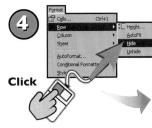

Click

Making a Row or Column Disappear

Hiding columns and rows is a good way to hide calculation columns or rows that aren't really critical for your audience to see. You also can hide other columns that you want to include in the worksheet, but don't want to display.

✓ **Unhide**
For information on how to unhide a column or row once it is hidden, see Task 19, "Unhiding Rows and Columns."

! **WARNING**
Hidden elements don't print when you print the worksheet.

✓ **Drag Hide**
You also can hide a column or row by dragging its right border past the left (column) or bottom border past the top (row).

---

1 Select any cell in the column you want to hide.

2 Choose **Format**, **Column**, **Hide**. Excel hides the column. You can tell whether the column is hidden by the jump in the lettering or numbering.

3 Select any cell in the row you want to hide.

4 Choose **Format**, **Row**, **Hide**. Excel hides the row. You can tell whether the row is hidden by the jump in the lettering or numbering.

End Task

Task 19: Unhiding Rows and Columns

Making a Row or Column Reappear

It's kind of tricky to unhide a row or column because you need a way to select the hidden row or column. Start by selecting rows or columns on either side, and then select the **Unhide** command.

Hide

For information on how to hide a column or row once it is hidden, see Task 18, "Hiding Rows and Columns."

Drag Unhide

You also can place the mouse pointer where the hidden row or column should appear. You have to adjust the mouse pointer carefully. When it is in the correct spot, it changes from a thick line to two thin lines, indicating the hidden column is selected. Drag to unhide the column or row.

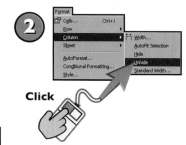

Click

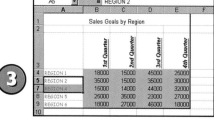

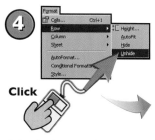

Click

1 Select the columns on both sides of the hidden column.

2 Choose **Format**, **Column**, **Unhide**. The column is unhidden.

3 Select the rows on both sides of the hidden row.

4 Choose **Format**, **Row**, **Unhide**. The row is unhidden.

Task 20: Using AutoFormat

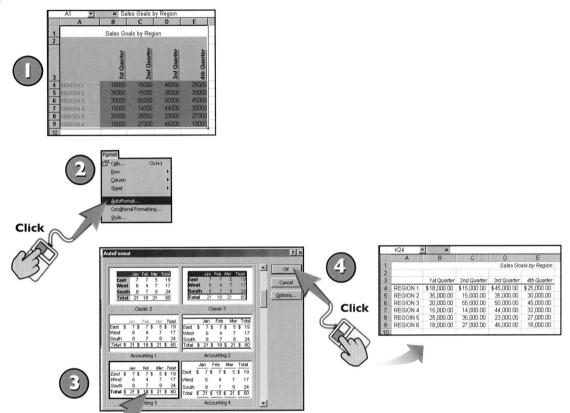

Click

Click

Click

Automatically Formatting Worksheets

Using all of the formatting capabilities discussed to this point, you could format your worksheets in a very effective and professional manner, but it might take a while to get good at it. In the meantime, Excel provides the AutoFormat feature, which can format selected cells using predefined formats. This feature is a quick way to format large amounts of data and provides ideas on how to format data.

① Select the cells you want to AutoFormat.

② Choose **Format**, **AutoFormat** to open the AutoFormat dialog box.

③ Click the AutoFormat you want (for example, **Accounting 3**) in the sample preview area.

④ Click the **OK** button to apply the AutoFormat to your data.

✓ Modifying AutoFormat

If you find a format in the AutoFormat tool that doesn't quite meet your requirements, you can use that format but then make any necessary changes directly in the worksheet.

Task 21: Using Conditional Formatting

Formatting Cells Based on Content

At times, you might want the formatting of a cell to depend on the value it contains. For this, use **Conditional Formatting,** which lets you specify up to three conditions that, when met, cause the cell to be formatted in the manner defined for that condition. If none of the conditions are met, the cell keeps its original formatting. For example, you can set a conditional format, such that if sales for a particular quarter exceed $40,000, the data in the cell will be red.

✓ Painting a Format onto Other Cells

You can copy the conditional formatting from one cell to another by using the Format Painter button. Click the cell whose formatting you want to copy. Then click the **Format Painter** button. Finally, drag over the cells to which you want to copy the formatting.

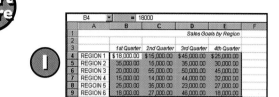

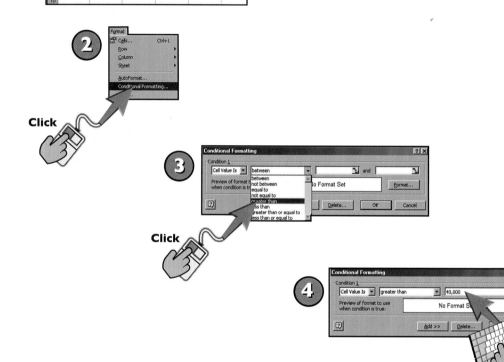

Click

Click

1 Select the cells you want to apply conditional formatting.

2 Choose **Format, Conditional Formatting** to open the Conditional Formatting dialog box.

3 Click the drop-down list to select the type of condition that the **Cell Value Is** (for example, **greater than**).

4 Type the value of the condition (for example, **40,000**).

Next Step

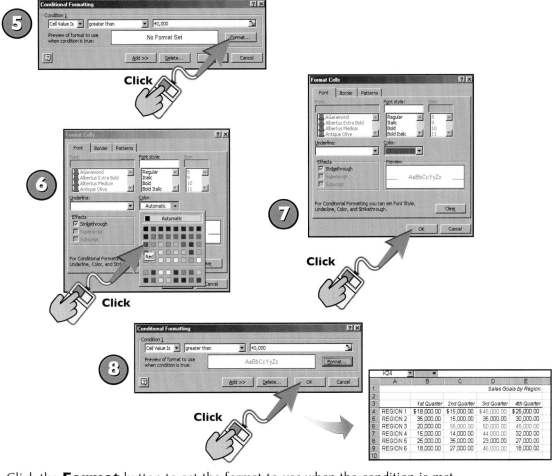

⑤ Click the **Format** button to set the format to use when the condition is met.

⑥ Click the options you want to set in the Format Cells dialog box (for example, the color **Red**).

⑦ Click the **OK** button to accept your formatting changes.

⑧ Click the **OK** button in the Conditional Formatting dialog box. Excel applies your formatting to any cells that meet the condition you specified.

When to Use Conditional Formatting
Use Conditional Formatting to draw attention to values that have different meanings depending on whether they are positive or negative, such as profit or loss values.

End Task

Task 22: Copying Formatting

Placing a Format Elsewhere

Copying formatting is a quick way to save time and effort. Suppose that you selected a range, added a border, changed the alignment, and used a different number format. You've got the range just how you want it. Now you want to use the same set of formats on another cell or range. Rather than redo all your work, you can copy the formats using the Format Painter button on the toolbar.

Click

✓ **Column Width and Row Height**
These formatting elements might not necessarily copy to the cells you want. If this happens, refer to Tasks 14 and 15.

 Select the cells that contain the formatting you want to copy.

 Click the **Format Painter** button on the Standard toolbar. The mouse pointer displays a little paintbrush next to the cross.

 Select the cells to which you want to copy the formatting. The formatting is applied to the selected range.

Task 23: Clearing Formatting

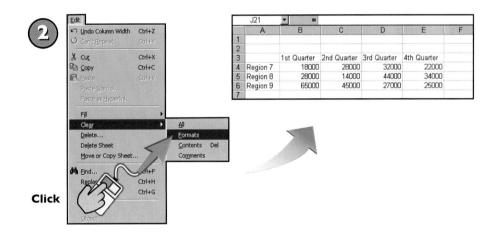

Click

Removing Cell Formatting

Sometimes you will go overboard, and your cell will be a mish-mash of formatting. If you want to clear the formatting and start over, you can do so.

1 Select the cell or range you want to clear.

2 Choose **Edit**, **Clear**, **Formats**. Excel clears all the formatting.

 Undo Clear
If you clear your formats and prefer them as they were, you can choose to Undo this clearing. Refer to Part 3, Task 3, "Undoing and Redoing Changes."

PART 5

Working with Formulas and Functions

In Excel, a **formula** calculates a value based on the values in other cells of the workbook. Excel displays the result of a formula in a cell as a numeric value.

Functions are abbreviated formulas that perform a specific operation on a group of values. Excel provides over 250 functions that can help you with tasks ranging from determining loan payments to calculating investment returns. For example, the SUM function is a shortcut for entering an addition formula. SUM is the name of the function that automatically adds entries in a range. First you type **=SUM(** in either lower- or uppercase letters. Then you select the range. You end the function by typing **)**, which also tells Excel you are finished selecting the range.

The way you refer to a cell in a formula determines how the formula is affected when you copy the formula into a different cell. You can use three types of cell references—relative, absolute, and mixed. The formulas you create in this section contain **relative cell references**. When you copy a formula from one cell to another, the relative cell references in the formula change to reflect the new location of the formula.

An **absolute cell reference** does not change when you copy the formula to a new cell. In certain formulas, you might want an entry to always refer to one specific cell value. For example, you might want to calculate the interest on several different principal amounts. The interest percentage remains unchanged, or absolute, so you designate the entry in the formula that refers to the interest percentage as an absolute cell reference.

A **mixed cell reference** is a single cell entry in a formula that contains both a relative and an absolute cell reference. A mixed cell reference is helpful when you need a formula that always refers to the values in a specific column but the values in the rows must change, and vice versa.

Tasks

Automatically Summing Cells

In a worksheet, if you want to show a sum of values from some cells you could add them yourself and type the total. But if you then change any of the values, the sum becomes inaccurate. Excel can use formulas to perform calculations for you. Because a formula refers to the cells rather than to the values, Excel updates the sum whenever you change the values in the cells.

✓ **Selecting Specific AutoSum Cells**

If you don't want to AutoSum on the cells Excel selects for you, you can click on the first cell you want, hold down the **Shift** key, and click on each additional cell you would like to include in the calculation. When you finish selecting the cells you want to calculate, press Enter to see the result.

Task 1: Using AutoSum

Start Here

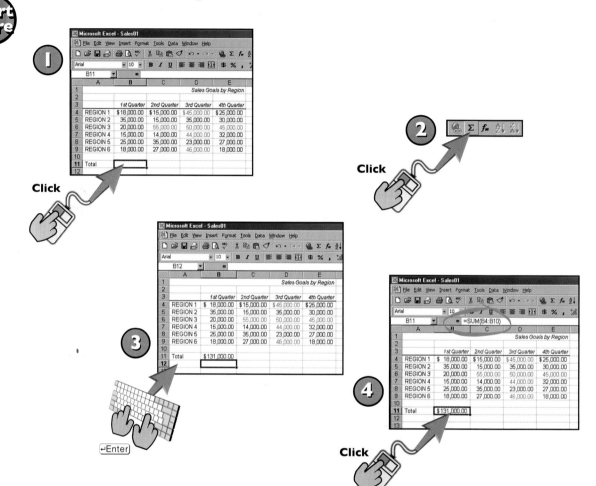

Click

Click

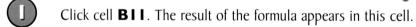

⏎Enter

Click

① Click cell **B11**. The result of the formula appears in this cell.

② Click the **AutoSum** button on the Standard toolbar. Excel selects the most obvious range of numbers to calculate and indicates this with a dotted line around the cells.

③ Press the **Enter** key to accept the range. Select alternative cells if necessary, refer to Part I, Task 5 on selecting cells.

④ Click cell **B11** to make it the active cell. Notice that the formula is displayed in the Formula Bar.

End Task

Task 2: Entering a Formula

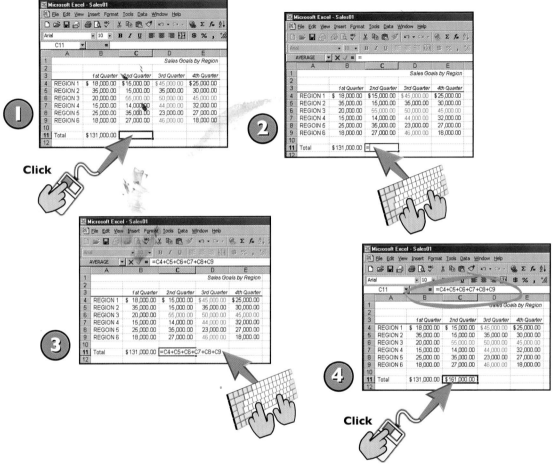

Click

Click

Typing Formulas

Sometimes you don't want to use AutoSum because you have specific cell references on which you want to perform calculations. In this instance, you can type the desired formula directly into the cell.

✓ **Canceling a Formula**
If you start to enter a formula and then decide you don't want to use it, you can skip entering the formula by pressing the **Esc** key.

✓ **Order of Operation**
Excel first performs any calculations within parentheses: (1+2)=3. Then it performs multiplication or division calculations from left to right: (12+24)/(3*2)=6. Finally, it performs any addition or subtraction from left to right: (12+24)/(3*2)–5=1.

(1) Click cell **C11**. The result of the formula appears in this cell.

(2) Type = (the equal sign).

(3) Type **C4+C5+C6+C7+C8+C9** and press the **Enter** key.

(4) Click cell **C11** to make it the active cell. Notice that the formula is displayed in the Formula Bar.

Task 3: Editing a Formula

Updating or Altering Formulas

After you enter a formula, you can change the values in the referenced cells, and Excel automatically recalculates the value of the formula based on the cell changes. You can include any cells in your formula; they do not have to be next to each other. Also, you can combine mathematical operations—for example, C3+C4–D5.

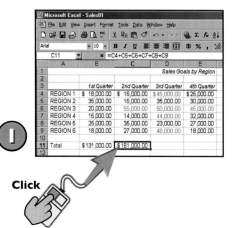

Click

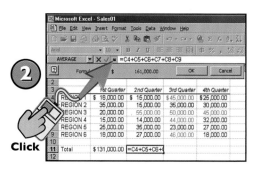

Click

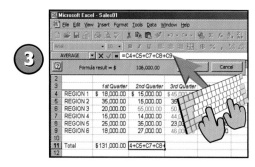

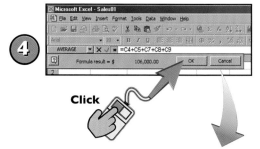

Click

✓ **Pressing F2**
Instead of using the Formula Bar to edit your formulas, you can press the F2 key and edit your formula just like you would regular text or data.

① Click cell **C11** to make it the active cell. Notice that the formula is displayed in the Formula Bar.

② Click the **Edit Formula** button (=).

③ Type or delete changes to your formula. For example, perhaps you don't want cell C6 because it has a conditional format assigned for a value of over 40,000 (refer to Part 4, Task 21).

④ Click the **OK** button. The changes are made and the result appears in the cell.

End Task

Task 4: Copying a Formula

Start Here

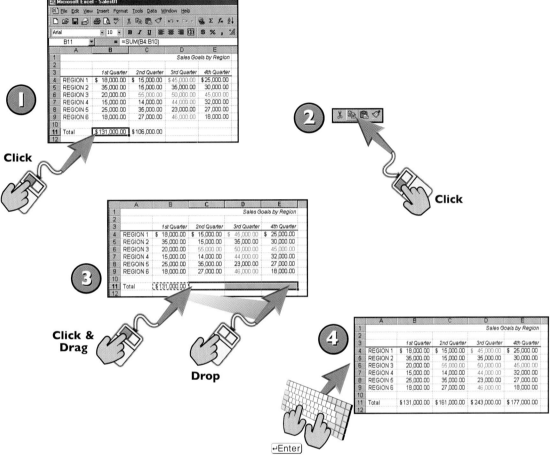

Click

Click

Click & Drag

Drop

①　Click the cell that contains the formula you want to copy (for example, **B11**).

②　Click the **Copy** button on the Standard toolbar.

③　Click and drag the mouse pointer over all the cells where you want to paste the function. A line surrounds the cell you are copying.

④　Press the **Enter** key to paste the formula into each of the specified cells.

Reusing a Formula

When you build your worksheet, you often use the same data and formulas in more than one cell. With Excel's Copy command, you can create the initial data or formula once and then place copies of this information in the appropriate cells. You do not have to go to each cell and enter the same formula.

✓ **List AutoFill**
List AutoFill automatically extends formatting and formulas in lists. For example, create a list with different fields in each column and totals in the bottom row and format the list in a consistent way (font size and color). If you add a new column to the right, Excel will fill in the formatting and total formula for you. See Part 4 for more about formatting cells.

✓ **Increase Cell Width**
If you paste a copied formula, you might need to alter the size of your columns or rows to accommodate the new size of the data in the cell. For example, you need to increase the width of columns **D** and **E**.

End Task

Task 5: Naming a Cell or Range

Assigning Special Names

You can create range names that make it easier to create formulas and move to that range. For example, a formula that reads Qrt1 is easier to understand than B4:B9. Not only is it easier to remember a name than the cell addresses, but Excel also displays the range name in the Name box—next to the Formula Bar. You can name a single cell or a selected range in the worksheet.

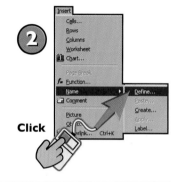

Click

Click

✓ Naming Ranges

Begin the range name with a letter or underscore. You can include upper- and lowercase letters and you can include as many as 255 characters. Don't use a range name that looks like a cell reference and don't include spaces.

1 Select the cell or range you want to name.

2 Choose **Insert**, **Name**, **Define** to open the Define Name dialog box, which displays the range coordinates and suggests a name.

3 Type the range name you want to use (for example, **Qtr1**).

4 Click the **OK** button. Excel names the range. When the range is selected, it appears in the Name box. Repeat these steps for any other range names you would like to assign.

Task 6: Using a Name in a Formula

Start Here

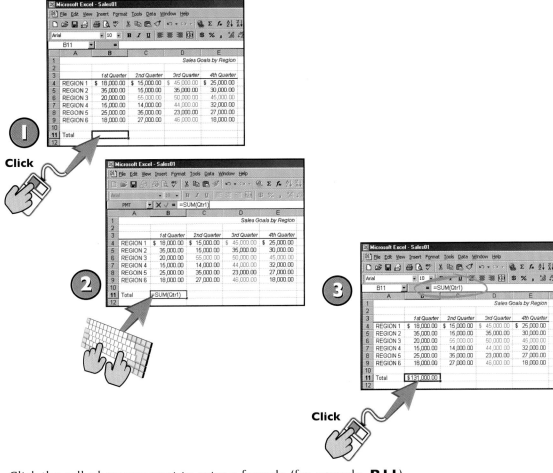

Click

Click

②

③

Referencing Names in Formulas

One of the reasons you create a name is so that you can easily refer to that cell or range in a formula. Rather than type or select a range or cell, type the name or select it from the **Paste Name** dialog box.

✔ **Paste Name**
If you forget the name of a range while you are typing a formula choose **Insert, Name, Paste** and place the range name automatically in the formula.

✔ **Go To a Named Range**
To go to a named range, choose **Edit, Go To**. Click on the range name in the list, and then click **OK**.

✔ **Deleting a Name**
To delete a name, choose **Insert, Name, Define**. In the Define Name dialog box, select the range you want to delete and then click the **Delete** button. Click **OK** to confirm the deletion.

① Click the cell where you want to enter a formula (for example, **B11**).

② Type the formula to find the Year Total using named quarter ranges (for example, `=SUM(Qtr1)`), and press the **Enter** key.

③ Click cell **B11** to make it the active cell. Notice that the formula is displayed in the Formula Bar.

End Task

Task 7: Finding a Cell Average

Entering an Average Function

A function is one of Excel's many built-in formulas for performing a specialized calculation on the data in your worksheet. For example, instead of totaling your sales data, maybe you want to know the average of each quarter per region (Average function).

✓ **Paste Function Dialog Box**
The Paste Function dialog box offers many functions. Practice using different functions and see the results you get from your calculations. As you experiment, you can move the Paste Function dialog box around or collapse it to see your cells.

✓ **Select Cells Yourself**
If Excel doesn't automatically select the cells you want, you can select them yourself by clicking in the first cell, holding down the Shift key, and clicking in the last cell.

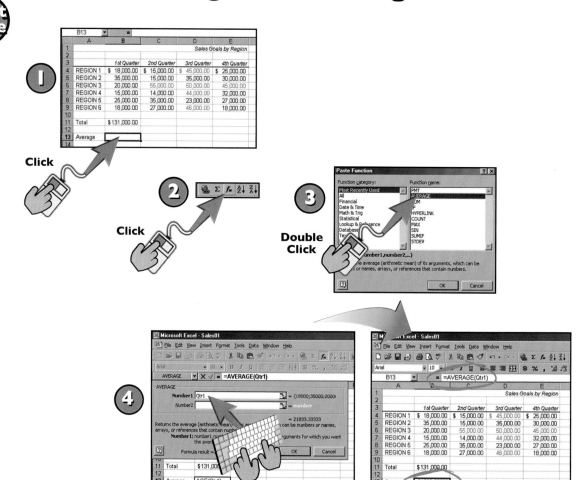

Click

Click

Double Click

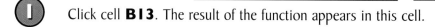

1 Click cell **B13**. The result of the function appears in this cell.

2 Click the **Paste Function** button on the Standard toolbar to open the Paste Function dialog box.

3 Double-click the **AVERAGE** option in the **Most Recently Used Function Category**, **Function Name** list box. Excel selects a range of cells it determines you want to average.

4 Type the cell range or range name (for example, **Qtr1**) and press the **Enter** key. The result appears in the active cell and the function is displayed in the Formula bar.

End Task

Task 8: Finding the Largest Cell Amount

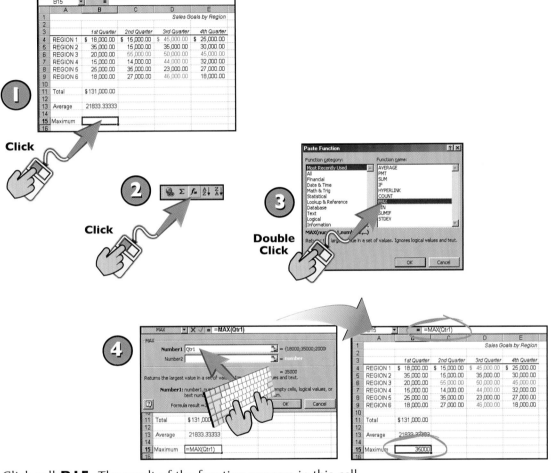

Click

Click

Double
Click

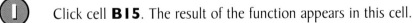

Entering a Maximum Function

A function is one of Excel's many built-in formulas for performing a specialized calculation on the data in your worksheet. For example, instead of totaling your sales data, maybe you want to know in which quarter you had the largest sales (Max function). This way you can reward your top regional sales.

1 Click cell **B15**. The result of the function appears in this cell.

2 Click the **Paste Function** button on the Standard toolbar to open the Paste Function dialog box.

3 Double-click the **MAX** option in the **Most Recently Used Function Category**, **Function Name** list box. Excel selects a range of cells it determines you want to average.

4 Type the cell range or range name (for example, **Qtr1**) and press the **Enter** key. The result appears in the active cell and the function is displayed in the Formula Bar.

✓ **Minimum Cell**
Besides finding the largest cell amount, you can find the smallest cell amount. See Task 10 for more information.

Task 9: Counting the Number of Cells That Meet a Requirement

Entering a Count If Function

A function is one of Excel's many built-in formulas for performing a specialized calculation on the data in your worksheet. For example, instead of totaling your sales data, maybe you want to know how many regional quarters were under $20,000.

✓ SUMIF Function
Another alternative to using If statements is to try using the **SUMIF** function. Basically, any cells that fit a particular criteria are added together. This is convenient when you are totaling sales numbers for separate products by product number.

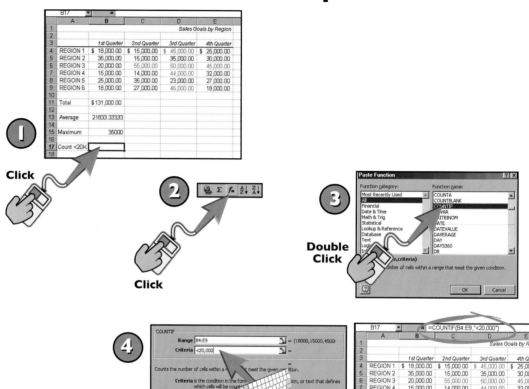

Start Here

Click

Click

Double Click

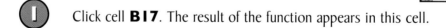

1 Click cell **B17**. The result of the function appears in this cell.

2 Click the **Paste Function** button on the Standard toolbar to open the Paste Function dialog box.

3 Double-click the **COUNTIF** option in the **All Function Category**, **Function Name** list box. Excel selects a range of cells it determines you want to average.

4 Type the cell range or range name **B4:E9**, press **Tab** and type **<20,000**; press the **Enter** key. The result is in the active cell and the function is displayed in the Formula Bar.

End Task

Task 10: Finding the Smallest Cell Amount

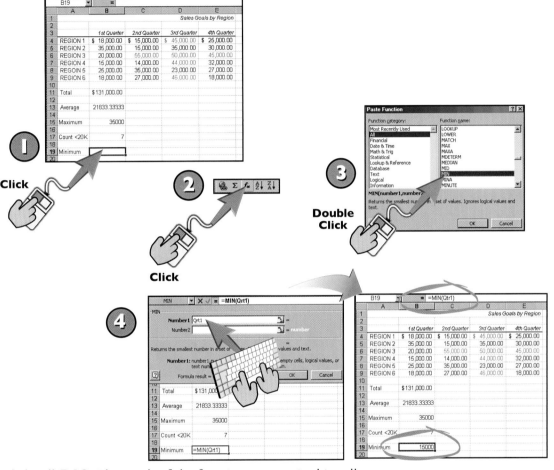

Click

Click

Double Click

Entering a Minimum Function

A function is one of Excel's many built-in formulas for performing a specialized calculation on the data in your worksheet. For example, instead of totaling your sales data, maybe you want to know in which quarter you had the lowest sales (Min function). This way you can know in which regions you need to improve.

1. Click cell **B19**. The result of the function appears in this cell.

2. Click the **Paste Function** button on the Standard toolbar to open the Paste Function dialog box.

3. Double-click the **MIN** option in the **All Function Category**, **Function Name** list box. Excel selects a range of cells it determines you want to average.

4. Type the cell range or range name (for example, **Qtr1**) and press the **Enter** key. The result appears in the active cell and the function is displayed in the Formula Bar.

✓ **Maximum Cell**
Besides finding the smallest cell amount, you can find the largest cell amount. See Task 8 for more information.

Task 11: Using AutoCalculate

Automatically Calculating Results

Perhaps you want to see a function performed on some of your data, such as finding out what the highest 4th Quarter sales were for all regions in the year 2000. But you don't want to add the function directly into the worksheet. Excel's AutoCalculate feature can help.

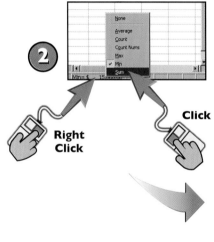

Start Here

Right Click

Click

✓ Turning AutoCalculate Off

You can turn the AutoCalculate feature off by selecting **None** from the AutoCalculate shortcut menu.

1 Select the cells that you want to AutoCalculate.

2 Right-click the status bar and choose **Sum** (to total the selection) from the shortcut menu. Excel will automatically calculate the cells and display the answer in the status bar.

End Task

Task 12: Filling a Complete Series

Start Here

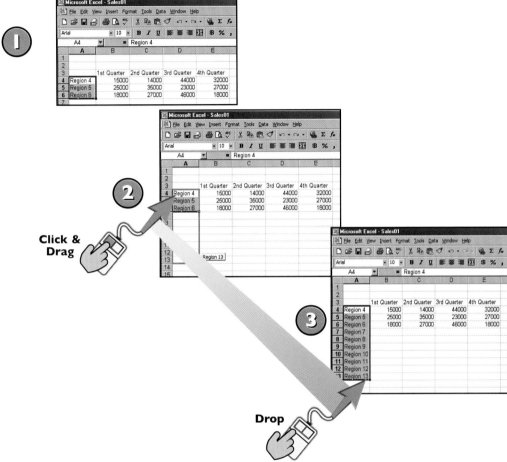

Click & Drag

Drop

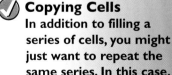

Using the AutoFill Command

Suppose cells that you want to AutoCalculate that you want to use a series of months as column heads. Do you have to type each month individually? Not with Excel. You can enter the first month and fill the remaining months across a selected range. You can use this technique to fill in a series of numbers, text entries, dates, and formulas.

1 Select the cell or cells that contain the entry.

2 Click and drag the fill handle in the lower-right corner of the cell. The pointer appears as a small cross, and you see ScrollTips for the entries as you drag.

3 Release the mouse button when you've filled the range you want. Excel fills the range with the selected series.

✓ **Copying Cells**
In addition to filling a series of cells, you might just want to repeat the same series. In this case, you will want to simply copy the cells. See Part 3, Task 9 for more information on copying cells.

End Task

Task 13: Fixing #### Errors

Understanding #### in a Cell

When a cell contains ####, the column is not wide enough to display the data. Widen the column to see the cell's contents.

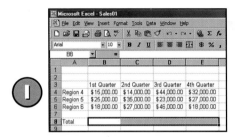

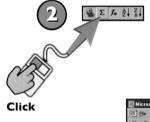

Click

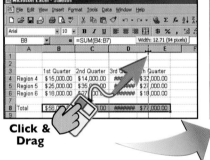

Click & Drag

✓ **Begin with Larger Columns**

It is a good idea to start out with columns larger than you need. Then you can decrease their size while you are formatting the worksheet.

① Select the cells in which you want to create totals.

② Click the **AutoSum** button on the Standard toolbar.

③ Click on the column **D** border and drag it to increase the size of the column width. The error disappears.

End Task

Task 14: Fixing #DIV/0! Errors

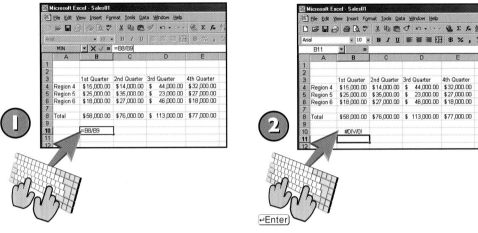

Dividing by Zero

When a cell contains #DIV/0!, the formula is trying to divide a number by 0 or an empty cell.

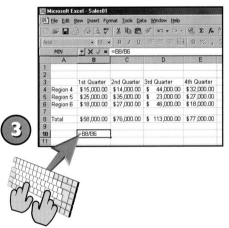

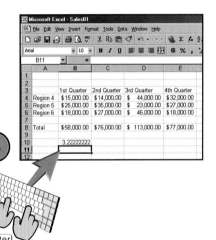

(1) Type a formula (for example, **=B8/B9**) in cell B10.

(2) Press the **Enter** key. You get the #DIV/0! error because this is not a correct calculation (there is nothing in cell B9, which defaults the cell value to 0).

(3) Click on cell **B10**, press **F2** on the keyboard, and retype the formula as **=(B8/B6)**.

(4) Press the **Enter** key. The error disappears.

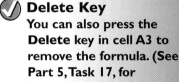

Delete Key
You can also press the **Delete** key in cell A3 to remove the formula. (See Part 5, Task 17, for instructions on getting rid of data.)

Task 15: Fixing #NAME? Errors

Recognizing Bad Cell References and Function Names

When a cell contains #NAME?, the formula contains incorrectly spelled cell or function names.

✅ **Paste Function**
See Task 3 to learn how to enter a function by using the Paste Function button on the Standard toolbar. This helps eliminate spelling errors in functions.

Start Here

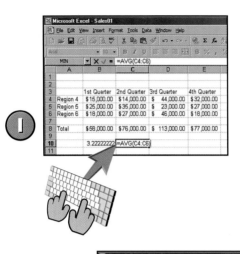

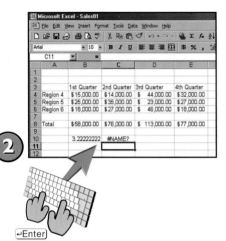

⏎Enter

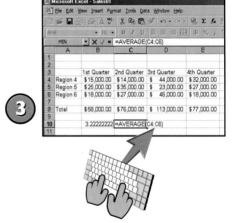

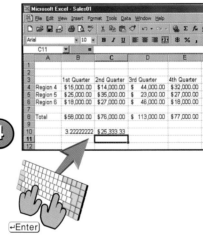

⏎Enter

① Type the formula you want to use in your calculation (for example, **=AVG(C4:C6)**) in cell C10.

② Press the **Enter** key. You get the #NAME? error because AVG is not the correct spelling for this function.

③ Click on cell **C10**, press **F2** on the keyboard, and retype the formula as **=AVERAGE(A1/A2)**.

④ Press the **Enter** key. The error disappears.

End Task

Task 16: Fixing #VALUE! Errors

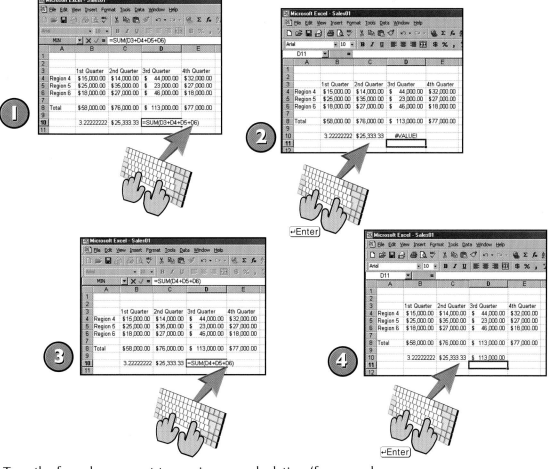

Recognizing a Value Problem

When a cell contains #VALUE!, the formula contains nonnumeric data or cell or function names that cannot be used in the calculation.

1 Type the formula you want to use in your calculation (for example, **=SUM(D3+D4+D5+D6))** in cell D10.

2 Press the **Enter** key. You get the #VALUE! error because the value in cell D3 is a textual value, not numeric.

3 Click on cell **D10**, press **F2** on the keyboard, and retype the formula as **=SUM(D4+D5+D6)**.

4 Press the **Enter** key. The error disappears.

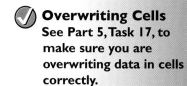

Overwriting Cells
See Part 5, Task 17, to make sure you are overwriting data in cells correctly.

End Task

Task 17: Recognizing the #REF! Error

Understanding Bad Cell References

When a cell contains #REF!, the formula contains a reference to a cell that isn't valid. Frequently, this means you deleted a referenced cell. The best solution is to undo your action and review the cells involved in the formula.

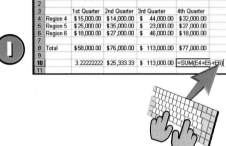

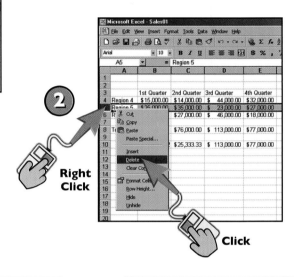

Right Click

Click

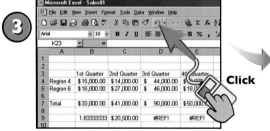

Click

✓ **Checking References**
If after you undo the #REF! error and you want to find out what caused it, see Tasks 19 and 20 for more information on checking formula and cell references.

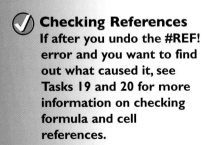

 Type the formula you want to use in your calculation, such as **=SUM(E4+E5+E6)** and press the **Enter** key.

 Right-click row header **5** and choose **Delete** from the shortcut menu. You get the #REF! error because the value in cell referenced in row 5 are no longer available in the formula.

 Click the **Undo** button. The error disappears.

End Task

Task 18: Recognizing Circular References

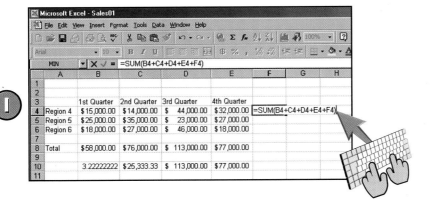

A Cell Can't Refer to Itself

A circular reference results when one of the cells you are referencing in your calculation is the cell in which you want the calculation to appear.

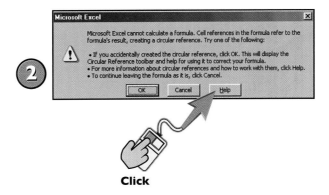

Click

① Type the formula you want to use in your calculation (for example, =SUM(B4+C4+D4+E4+F4)) and press the **Enter** key.

② Choose one of the following in the Microsoft Excel message box: the **OK** button to create a circular reference, the **Cancel** button to edit and correct your formula, or the **Help** button to help you create and understand circular references.

Circular Reference Toolbar

If you didn't intend to create a circular reference and you chose **OK** in the message box, the Circular Reference toolbar and Help will appear to assist you in correcting your actions.

Task 19: Checking for Formula References

Tracing Precedents

One way to check a formula is to select that formula and then trace all cells that are referenced in that formula. Cells that are referenced are called *precedents*.

✓ **Moving References**
You can double-click the arrows to move from one reference to another.

✓ **Other Auditing Commands**
You also can select the Auditing commands by selecting **Tools, Auditing**, and then selecting the command you want from the submenu.

✓ **Close Toolbar**
Close the Auditing Toolbar by clicking the **Close** button (**X**) in the upper-right corner of the toolbar.

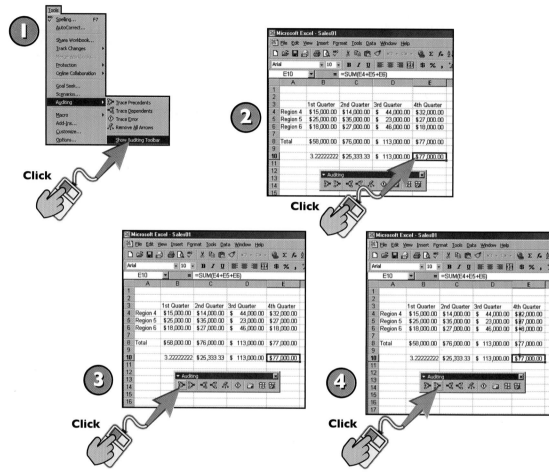

Start Here

Click

Click

Click

Click

1 Choose **Tools**, **Auditing**, **Show Auditing Toolbar**. You see the toolbar onscreen.

2 Click the cell you want to trace. This cell must contain a formula.

3 Click the **Trace Precedents** button. Excel draws tracer arrows to the appropriate cells.

4 Click the **Remove Precedents Arrows** button to remove the arrows.

End Task

Task 20: Checking for Cell References

Start Here

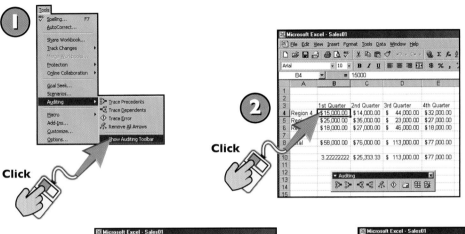

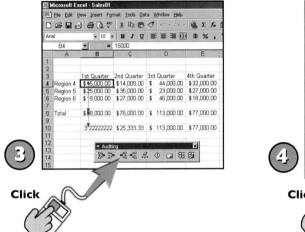

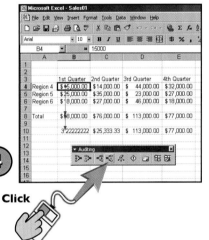

Tracing Dependents

When you trace a dependent, you start with a cell that is referenced in a formula and then trace all cells that reference this cell. This is another way to check formulas.

✓ **Close Toolbar**
Close the Auditing Toolbar by clicking the **Close** button (**X**) in the upper-right corner of the toolbar.

✓ **No References**
If the cell is not referenced in a formula, you see an error message saying so.

✓ **Using Trace Error**
If the cell contains an error message, use the **Trace Errors** button to have Excel trace possible reasons for the error.

① Choose **Tools**, **Auditing**, **Show Auditing Toolbar**. You see the toolbar onscreen.

② Click the cell you want to trace. This cell must *not* contain a formula.

③ Click the **Trace Dependents** button until you hear a beep that all the dependents have been traced. Excel displays tracer arrows to the appropriate cells.

④ Click the **Remove Dependents Arrows** button enough times to remove all the arrows (or click the **Remove All Arrows** button).

End Task

Working with Charts and Graphics

You've already learned the fundamentals of creating a worksheet. Now you can concentrate on some of the other features that add to the data presentation. For example, you can create a chart based on data in a worksheet. Charts are very useful for interpreting data; however, different people look at data in different ways. To account for this, you can quickly change the appearance of charts in Excel by clicking directly on the chart. You can change titles, legend information, axis points, category names, and more.

The **axes** are the grid on which the data is plotted. On a 2D chart, the y-axis is the vertical axis on a chart (**value axis**), and the x-axis is the horizontal axis (**category axis**). A 3D chart has three axes (add a z-axis). You can control all the aspects of the axes—the appearance of the line, the tick marks, the number format used, and more.

You can also draw on a chart or in a worksheet using one of several drawing tools, add a picture, and move and resize all these elements. Charts, pictures, clip art, and drawn items are all considered graphic **objects**.

Tasks

Task 1: Creating a Chart

Graphing Your Data

Numeric data can
sometimes be difficult to
interpret. Using data to
create charts helps visualize
the data's significance. For
example, you might not
have noticed that the same
month out of every year
has low sales figures, but it
becomes obvious when you
make a chart from the
data. The chart's visual
nature also helps others
review your data without
pouring over every number.

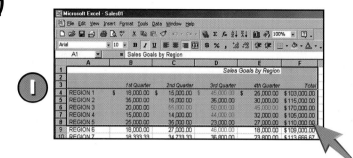

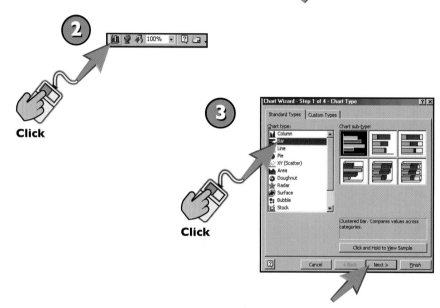

Click

Click

✓ **Click and Hold to
   View Sample**

The first step of the Chart
Wizard enables you to
select how your data will
look with a particular
chart type and sub-type.
You can see how the chart
will look by clicking on the
Click and Hold to View
Sample button.

1   Select the cells you want to place in your chart.

2   Click the **Chart Wizard** button on the Standard toolbar.

3   Click the **Chart type** (for example, **Bar**) and **Chart sub-type** in the Chart Wizard
dialog box; then choose **Next**.

Next
Step

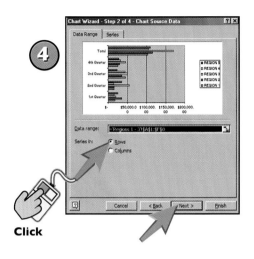

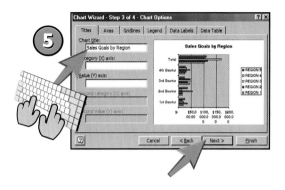

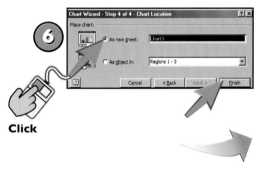

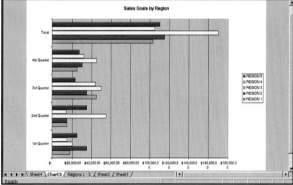

Click

Click

④ Click **Rows** (or **Columns**) to choose which data to base the chart on; then choose **Next**.

⑤ Type the various Titles for the chart (for example, **Sales Goals by Region**); then choose **Next**.

⑥ Click the option for where you want to place the chart (for example, choose **As new sheet**, titled **Chart3**); then choose **Finish**.

Task 2: Changing the Chart Type

Selecting a Different Chart

Charting is one of those skills you learn by doing. At first, you might not even know the type of chart you want until you see it. You can always select a different chart type for a chart so that it better represents the data.

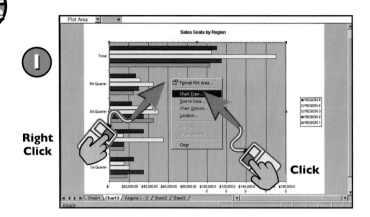

Right Click

Click

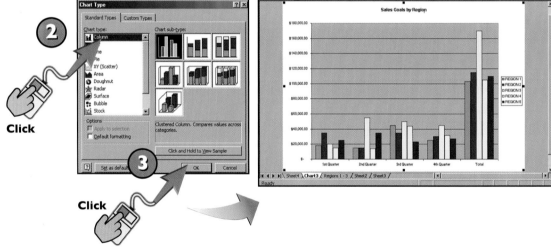

Click

Click

✅ **Default Chart Type**
The default chart type is a column chart. To make another chart type the default, select it in the Chart Type dialog box and then click the **Set as default chart** button.

1 Right-click the **Plot Area** and choose **Chart Type** from the shortcut menu.

2 Select the alternate Chart type and Chart sub-type (for example, **Column – Clustered Column**) in the Chart Type dialog box.

3 Click the **OK** button. The updated chart type appears in your chart.

Task 3: Altering Source Data Range

Start Here

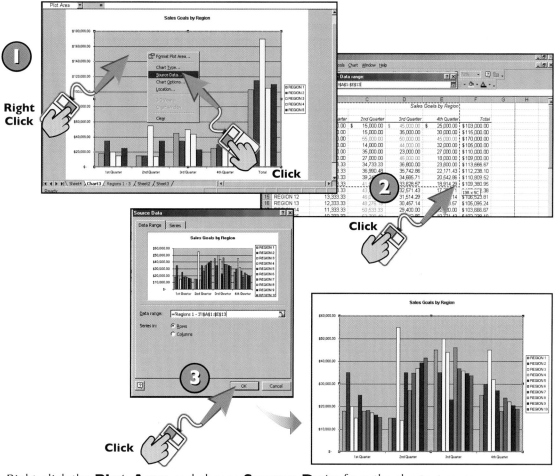

I Right Click

Click

Click

2

3

Click

Changing the Charted Information

Many times you will create a chart and then determine that you want to add more data series to your chart to include more information. When this is the case, you can easily add series to your chart by altering the source data you select in your original worksheet.

I Right-click the **Plot Area** and choose **Source Data** from the shortcut menu.

2 Click directly in your worksheet and select the data range you want. The **Data range** area automatically updates with the cells you selected.

3 Click the **OK** button in the Source Data dialog box. The updated data range appears in your chart.

⚠ WARNING

If you notice that one of the data points in your chart is way off scale, this is a good sign that you might have entered data into your worksheet incorrectly. If this is the case, edit the worksheet data and the chart will update automatically. Also refer to Task 8 on altering the original data.

End Task

Adding and Removing Chart Elements

Changing your chart options can be as much fun as creating the chart in the first place. You can add or edit your chart titles, alter your axes, add or remove gridlines, move or delete your legend, add or remove data labels, and even show the data table containing your original data.

Task 4: Altering Chart Options

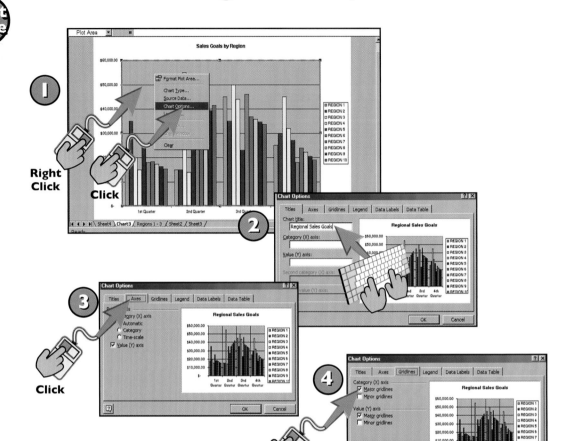

✓ **Double-click the Chart**

One of the fastest ways to edit charting options is to double-click directly on the element in the chart you want to alter. The appropriate dialog box opens and you can alter the chart options.

1 Right-click the **Plot Area** and choose **Chart Options** from the shortcut menu.

2 Type in a new **Chart title** (for example, **Regional Sales Goals**) on the Titles tab.

3 Click the **Axes** tab and see how altering the **Primary Axis** affects your chart.

4 Click the **Gridlines** tab and select to add **Category (X) axis Major gridlines**.

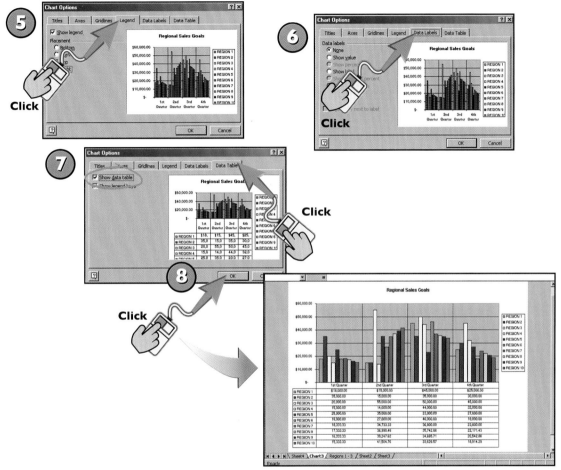

Axes Gridlines
To change the pattern and scale of the gridlines, double-click the gridline itself. Then use the Format Gridlines dialog box to make your selections. Click **OK**.

Legend
To change the font or pattern used in the legend, double-click the legend itself. Then use the Format Legend dialog box that appears to select a pattern and font.

Data Labels
If you want to show a data table along with the chart, click the **Data Table** tab in the Chart Options dialog box. Then click the **Show data table** check box and click **OK**.

5 Click the **Legend** tab and see how altering the **Placement** affects your chart.

6 Click the **Data Labels** tab and see how altering the **Data Labels** affects your chart.

7 Click the **Data Table** tab and select to **Show data table**.

8 Click the **OK** button to accept your chart options and see how your chart has changed.

Task 5: Formatting the Plot Area

Altering the Plot Area

The plot area consists of a border and an area. You can alter the style, color, and weight of the border. You can also alter the color of the plot area.

✓ Areas

If you are unsure whether you are in the Chart Area or the Plot Area, click directly on the chart. A ScreenTip appears telling you what area you are in. Or, you can refer to the Name Box.

✓ Border Type

If you want to alter your border type, be careful not to overpower the chart with lines that are too thick. This can take the attention away from the data.

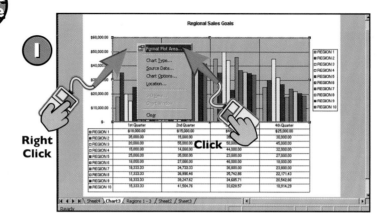

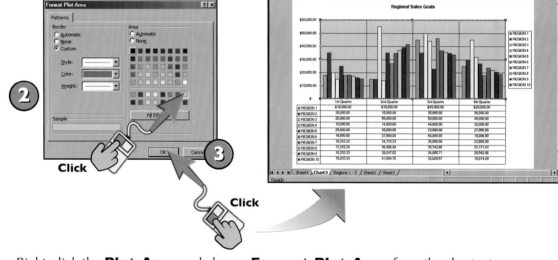

1 Right-click the **Plot Area** and choose **Format Plot Area** from the shortcut menu.

2 Select the **Area** color on the Patterns tab of the Format Plot Area dialog box.

3 Click the **OK** button to see how your chart has changed.

Task 6: Formatting the Chart Area

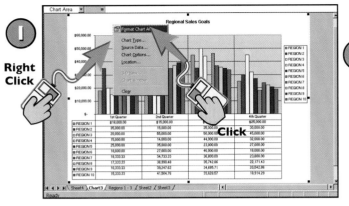

Right Click

Click

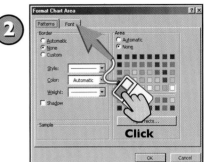

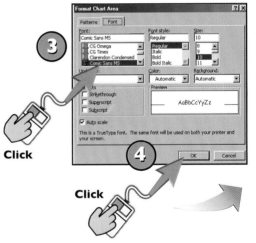

Click

Click

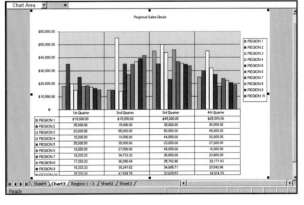

Altering the Chart Area

The chart area consists of a border, the area, and all the chart fonts. You can alter the style, color, and weight of the border. You can also alter the color of the plot area and change all the fonts and font styles in the chart.

Areas
If you are unsure whether you are in the **Chart Area** or the **Plot Area**, click directly on the chart. A ScreenTip appears telling you what area you are in. Or, you can refer to the Name Box.

Patterns
You can alter the background color of your chart just like you did in Task 5 when you changed your Area color. Refer to that task for more information.

 Right-click the **Chart Area** and choose **Format Chart Area** from the shortcut menu.

 Click the **Font** tab of the Format Chart Area dialog box.

 Select the Font options you would prefer (for example, the font Comic Sans MS).

 Click the **OK** button to see how your chart has changed.

Task 7: Formatting an Axis Scale

Altering Axis Increments

Excel automatically establishes the axis increments according to the maximum amount on the chart. Usually this will suffice, but if you want to show more detail about actual numbers, it can be convenient to alter your value axis.

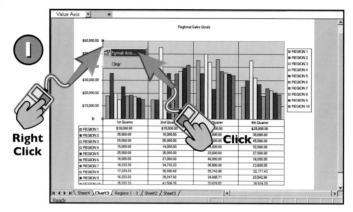

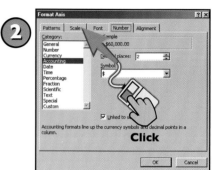

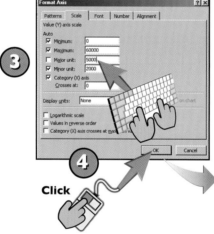

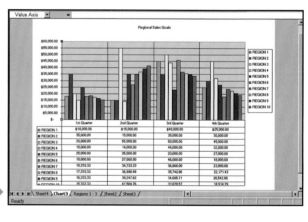

✓ **Number and Alignment**
To change the number format, click the **Number** tab. Select the numeric format you want to use. To change the alignment, click the **Alignment** tab. Select a rotation for the axes.

① Right-click the **Value Axis** and choose **Format Axis** from the shortcut menu.

② Click the **Scale** tab of the Format Axis dialog box.

③ Type **5000** for the **Major unit**, instead of 10000.

④ Click the **OK** button to see how your chart has changed.

Task 8: Altering the Original Data

Start Here

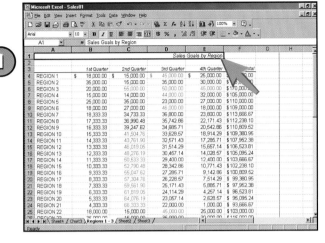

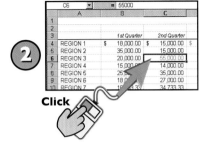

Click

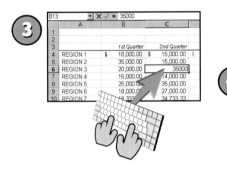

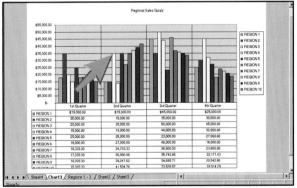

The chart is linked to the worksheet data, so when you make a change in the worksheet, the chart is updated. If you want to change a value in the worksheet, edit it as you do normally. The chart will be updated to reflect the change instantly. If you delete data in the worksheet, the matching data series will be deleted in the chart.

1 Select the worksheet or range that contains the charted data.

2 Click a cell that you want to alter or need to update.

3 Type in the new data and press the **Enter** key.

4 Go back to the chart and see how the data point has changed your chart.

✓ **Save Changes**
Make sure that you save your changes to a worksheet and chart often. You wouldn't want to lose any changes you made in case your network goes down or your computer freezes.

End Task

Task 9: Using Drawing Tools

Adding Arrows and Text Boxes

Excel has drawing tools that you can use to add to a worksheet or *chart sheet* (what a worksheet is called when it contains only a chart). In this task you are going to learn the advantages of using Excel's drawing tools to help point out information on a chart. Keep in mind that you can put these objects in a regular worksheet as well.

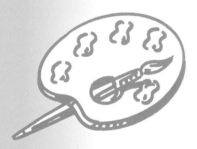

Start Here

Click

Click

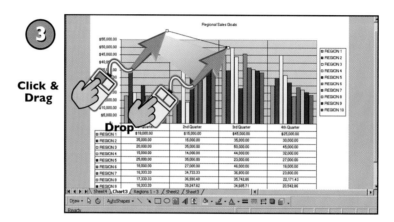

Click & Drag

Drop

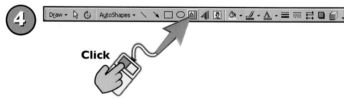

Click

✓ **Color and Style**
You also can use the Line Color and Line Style buttons to change the color and style of the lines used to draw the rectangle.

1 Click the **Drawing** button on the Standard toolbar. The Drawing toolbar appears as default above the status bar.

2 Click the **Arrow** button on the Drawing toolbar. The mouse pointer turns into a cross, which means you can begin to draw your arrow line.

3 Click and drag the line in the chart and release the left mouse button at the length you want the arrow.

4 Click the **Text Box** button on the Drawing toolbar. The mouse pointer turns into an insertion pointer, which means you can begin to draw your text box.

Next Step

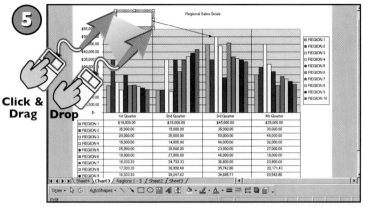

Click & Drag **Drop**

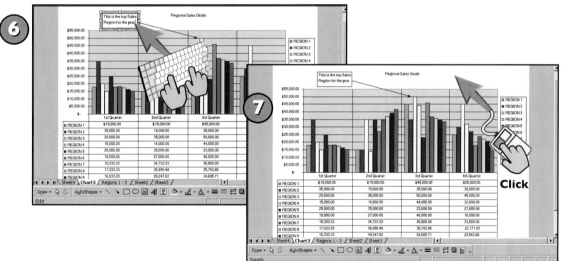

Click

⑤ Click and drag the text box in the chart and release the left mouse button at the size you want the box.

⑥ Type the text you want to enter in the text box.

⑦ Click anywhere outside the chart area to see how your drawings look.

✅ **AutoShapes**
The Drawing toolbar includes tools for drawing common shapes, such as a line, circle, square, and so on. If you aren't much of an artist or if you want to try some prefab symbols, insert an **AutoShape**. You can select from several lines, connectors, basic shapes, arrows, flowchart symbols, stars, callouts, banners, and more.

✅ **Modify Drawing Objects**
A drawn object is just like a picture—you can resize, move, and delete it. To resize: click on the object to see the sizing handles, drag the sizing handles to the size you want, and release the mouse button. To move: click on the object and drag it to the desired location in the worksheet. To delete: click on the object and press the **Delete** key on the keyboard.

Task 10: Inserting Clip Art

Adding Graphics to Worksheets

When you use Excel to generate reports or create presentation material, you might want to add some clip art graphics to improve the report's appearance or draw attention to a particular part of a worksheet. Excel provides many pictures from which you can choose.

Start Here

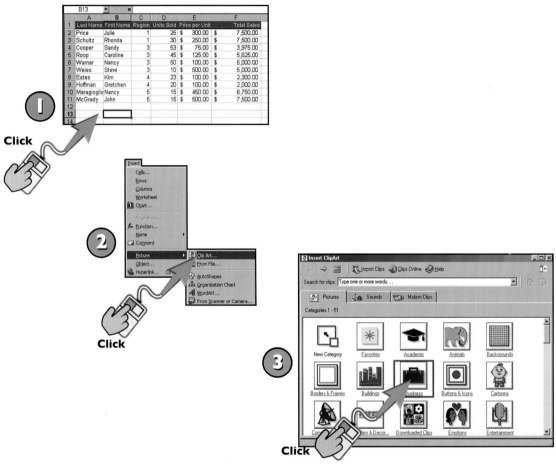

Click

Click

Click

✓ **Insert ClipArt Dialog Box**
You can leave this dialog box open if you need to insert more than one piece of clip art. In addition, you can use this dialog box to add sounds and movie clips.

 Click the cursor in the worksheet near where you want the clip art to appear.

 Choose **Insert**, **Picture**, **Clip Art** to open the Insert ClipArt dialog box.

 Click on the category of clip art in the Pictures tab (for example, **Business**) and scroll through the options.

Next Step

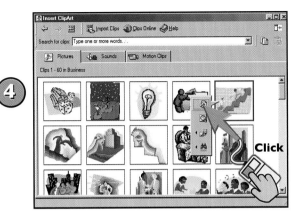

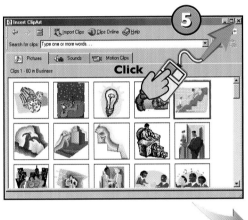

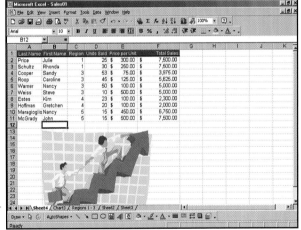

Click on the piece of clip art and choose **Insert clip** from the shortcut menu, which will insert the clip art into your worksheet.

Click the **X** button to close the Insert ClipArt dialog box.

Picture Toolbar
When you select a picture, the Picture toolbar appears with tools you can use to crop the picture, add a border to it, or adjust its brightness and contrast.

Format Picture
You can double-click on a picture to open the Format Picture dialog box. This enables you to alter the size, layout, colors and lines, and more.

Task 11: Selecting Objects

Choosing Different Objects

As you have seen so far in this part, you can add charts to a worksheet, draw objects, or insert pictures. Each of these items is a separate layer over the worksheet and is generically called an *object*. You can move, resize, and delete the object, as you will find in the following tasks. First, you need to select the object you want to modify.

✓ **Selecting Multiple Objects**

To select multiple objects, click the first object, and then press and hold down the **Shift** key and click on the second object. Continue doing this until all the objects you want are selected.

✓ **Reselect**

If you select a cell by accident, be sure to put the pointer right on the edge of the drawing. You also can click the **Select Object** button and then click the object.

Start Here

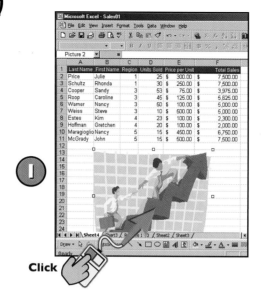

1

Click

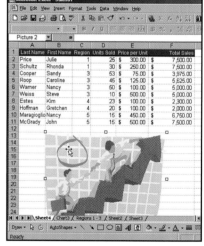

2

1 Click the object you want to change (for example, the clip art you inserted in Task 10). You see selection handles around the edges of that object.

2 Move the mouse pointer over the object and notice how it becomes a four-headed arrow.

End Task

Task 12: Resizing Objects

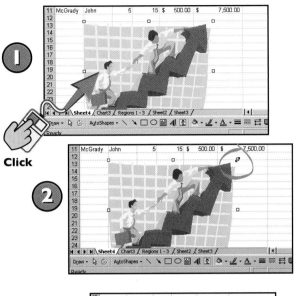

Click

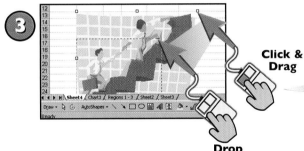

Click & Drag

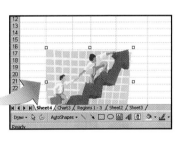

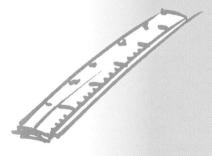

Drop

Changing the Size of an Object

If an object is too big (or too small), change the size. You can modify any type of object including a picture you have added, a chart, or a drawn object. In addition, you can continue to resize the object over and over until it is the size you want.

✓ **Corners Versus Sides**
You might notice that there are selection handles on the object corners and sides. The sides increase or decrease the height or width of an object, but the corners increase or decrease the height and width of an object at the same time.

① Click the object you want to resize (for example, the clip art you inserted in Task 10). You see selection handles around the edges of that object.

② Move the pointer over one of the selection handles. When the pointer is in the right spot, it changes to a two-headed arrow.

③ Click on the handle, drag the selection handles, and release the mouse button at the desired object size. The object is resized.

End Task

Task 13: Moving Objects

Changing the Location of an Object

When you draw or add an object, you might not like its placement. Perhaps you can't see the worksheet data, or perhaps you drew something on the worksheet but need to move it a little closer (or farther away). You can easily move an object.

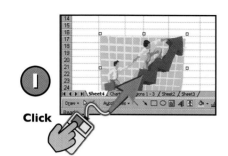

Click

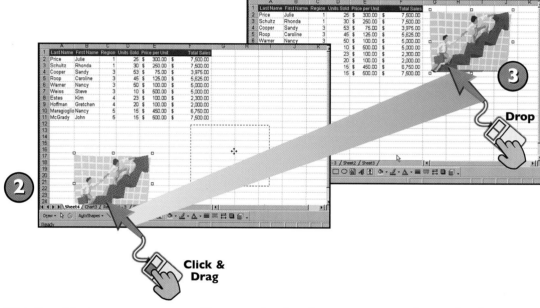

Drop

③

②

Click & Drag

 Cutting Objects
To copy an object, hold down **Ctrl** key and drag a copy off from the original.

 Move to Another Sheet or Workbook
To move the object to another sheet or workbook, select the object and then click **Edit, Cut.** Move to the new sheet or workbook and select the **Edit, Paste** command.

① Click the object you want to move (for example, the clip art you inserted in Task 10). You see selection handles around the edges of that object.

② Click directly on the object or its border (not the selection handles) and hold the left mouse button while dragging the object to the new location.

③ Release the mouse button to drop the object in the new location. The object is moved.

 End Task

Task 14: Deleting Objects

Start Here

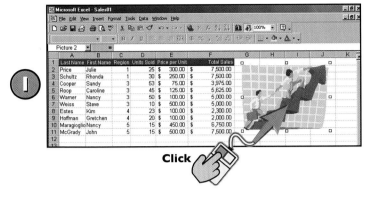

Click

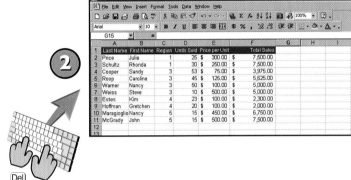

Del

End Task

Removing an Object from a Worksheet

If you add an object and no longer want to include it, you can delete it. As you experiment with charts, drawings, and pictures, you may go overboard, or you might make a mistake and want to start over. In any case, you can delete an object, as described here.

① Select the object you want to delete (for example, the clip art you inserted in Task 10). You see selection handles around the edges of that object.

② Press the **Delete** key on the keyboard. Excel deletes the object.

✓ **Undo Delete**
If you delete something by accident, click the **Undo** button on the Standard toolbar to undo the deletion.

Working with Data Lists

You can use Excel for more than totaling numbers. You also can use the program as a simple data management program. You can keep track of clients, products, orders, expenses, and more. You can set up a data list and use some of Excel's data list features, including sorting, subtotaling, and filtering.

Tasks

Task 1: Setting Up a Data List and Form

Creating a Data List and Form

A *data list* is a set of related information about a particular person, transaction, or event. One piece of information is a *field*, and one set of fields is called a *record*. In an Excel data list, you enter the column headings for the fields, and the records in the rows. One way to enter these records is by using a data list *form*.

✓ **Unique Names**
Be sure to use unique names for each column. Excel can get confused if you use the same name in more than one column.

✓ **Format Data List**
The database is an ordinary worksheet. You use the same procedure to make editing and formatting changes. You don't have to format your data list. Although, it will be more helpful while you are learning if you can see the full name of the data labels on which you are entering information.

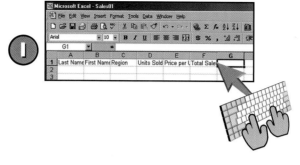

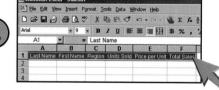

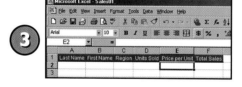

1 Type the headings for the columns of information (for example, `Last Name`, `First Name`, `Region`, `Units Sold`, `Price per Unit`, and `Total Sales`).

2 Select all the headers and format them with the **Classic 2 AutoFormat**. Refer to Part 4, Task 20 for more information on applying AutoFormat to your data.

3 Format cell **E2** so that it has the Currency style. Refer to Part 4, Task 4 for more information.

4 Type the formula `=SUM(D2*E2)` into cell **F2** to calculate the **Units Sold** by the **Price per Unit** to equal the **Total Sales**. Refer to Part 5, Task 2 for more information.

Next Step

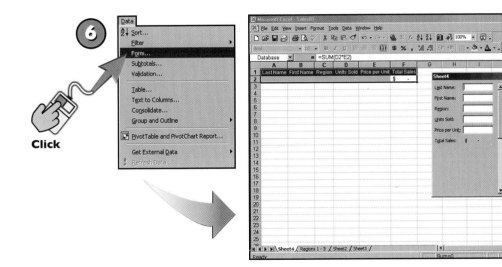

Click

Excel Message
If you don't select a row of cells along with your data list labels, Excel will prompt you with a message box asking you to specify the data list labels.

Total Sales
Notice how this area of the data form doesn't allow you to enter information. This is because it is a calculated field. To keep from entering invalid data into particular fields, create validation rules. More information on this in Task 3 "Adding Data Validation."

Close Form
You can close the data list form by clicking the **Close** button on the form.

5 Select the cells you want to establish the data list (for example, **A1:F2**).

6 Choose **Data**, **Form**. This tells Excel that you want your selected cells to be used as the data labels. The form will appear ready to enter data.

Task 2: Entering Data with a Form

Entering Records

If you like the regular worksheet style of entering data, you can enter data directly in the cells. Select each field and type an entry. Do this for each record in the database. If you prefer to concentrate on one record at a time, you can display a data form onscreen and enter the records in that form (as covered in this task).

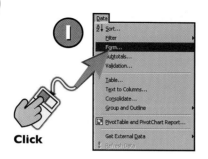

Click

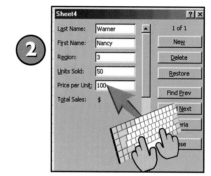

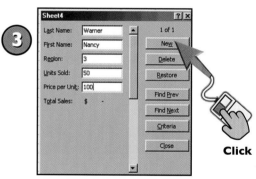

Click

 Manually Editing Entries

To edit a record in the worksheet, double-click the cell you want to edit, make the change, and press **Enter**. Otherwise, Task 5 shows you how to modify a data list entry with a form.

1 Choose **Data, Form** to open the data form for the worksheet data list you created in Task 1 (unless you still have it open).

2 Type the data for the first record into the data form (for example, **Warner, Nancy, 3, 50, 100**) pressing the Tab key between each field on the form.

3 Click the **New** button on the data list form. The data is automatically placed in your data list and the data form is ready for another entry.

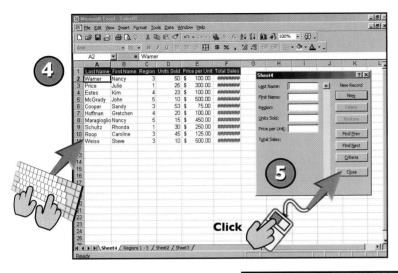

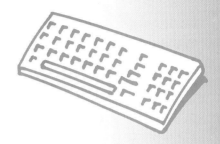

Click

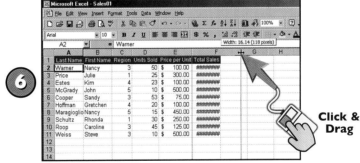

Click & Drag

✓ **Record Order**
You don't have to enter records in any particular order. You can later sort or filter your records so that they appear as you need. See Tasks 7 and 8 for more information.

✓ **Correcting Typos**
If you make an error when typing your records and you are still working on that record in the form, you can click the mouse pointer into the field in error and use the Delete and Backspace keys while editing your entry.

4 Type in around 10 data list entries using steps 2 and 3.

5 Click the **Close** button on the form to return to working in your worksheet data list.

6 Increase the width of the **Total Sales** column so you can see the totals onscreen. Refer to Part 4, Task 16 for more information on changing column width.

End Task

Checking Your Entries

You might find that while tediously entering records into your data list, you inadvertently make some mistakes. For example, your company only has 50 Sales Regions and you keep accidentally entering in numbers that couldn't possibly be an actual Sales Region, for example, 55. By setting up data validation *rule*, Excel automatically tells you when you have made this type of error.

Task 3: Adding Data Validation

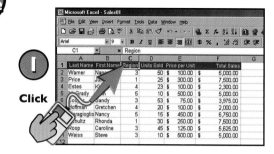

Click

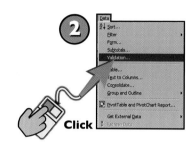

Click

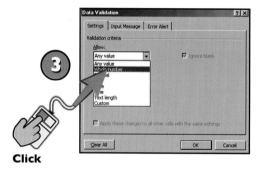

Click

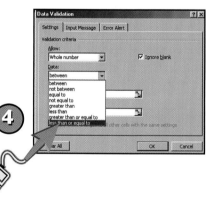

Click

✓ **Data List Form Open**
To open the data list form at any time, you must have the active cell be somewhere within the data list.

① Click a cell anywhere in the data list field that you want to apply data validation to (for example, **Region**).

② Choose **Data**, **Validation** to open the Data Validation dialog box.

③ Click **Whole number** from the **Allow** drop-down list box of the Validation criteria. This is because our Sales Regions will always be whole numbers.

④ Click **less than or equal to** from the **Data** drop-down list box of the Validation criteria. The Sales Regions will always be less than or equal to the total number of Regions.

Next Step

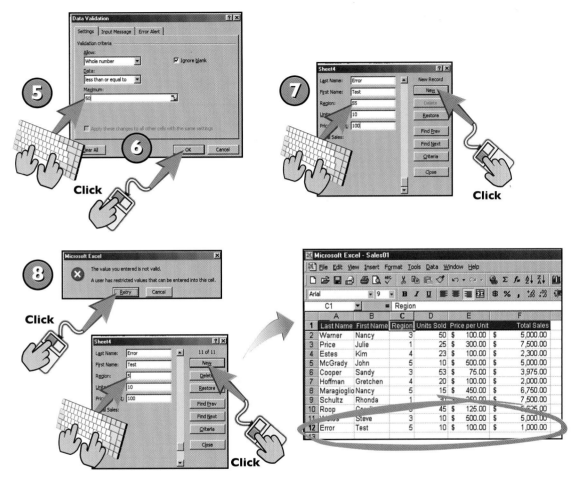

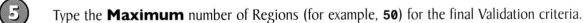

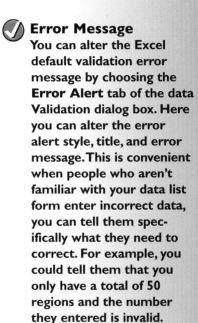

Error Message
You can alter the Excel default validation error message by choosing the **Error Alert** tab of the data Validation dialog box. Here you can alter the error alert style, title, and error message. This is convenient when people who aren't familiar with your data list form enter incorrect data, you can tell them specifically what they need to correct. For example, you could tell them that you only have a total of 50 regions and the number they entered is invalid.

Input Messages
In addition to validation rules and error messages, you can add input messages directly into your data list. This looks like a permanently viewable comment in your data list. For example, you could tell the person entering data that the Region field only accepts whole values between 1 and 50. This way they will think twice before they enter an invalid number.

---

5 Type the **Maximum** number of Regions (for example, **50**) for the final Validation criteria.

6 Click the **OK** button to accept your validation rules with Excel's default validation error message.

7 Type in a new data list record using the steps in Task 2 but add an incorrect entry in the Region field (for example, **55**), then click the **New** button.

8 Click the **Retry** button on the error message to return to the invalid record entry; type a correct Region field (for example, **5**) and try clicking the **New** button again. The record will be accepted.

Task 4: Finding a Record

Searching for a Particular Data List Record

Rather than wasting time trying to look through each record in a database to find the one you want, search for the record. You can limit the search to a specific field using the data form. For example, if you are trying to find information on a particular sales represent-ative, you could search on their last name.

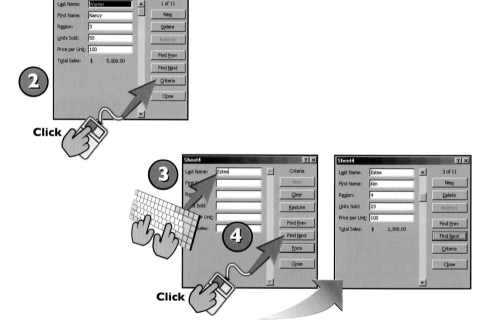

✓ No Match

If Excel can't find a match, you'll hear a beep, and Excel will return to the data form. Check your spelling. Rather than typing the entire value, type a partial value or use a comparison formula.

✓ Scroll Search

In addition to looking through the data list and using criteria to locate a record on your data list form, you can scroll through the list of records on your form.

1 Choose **Data**, **Form** to open the data form for the worksheet data list you created in Task I (unless you still have it open).

2 Click the **Criteria** button. The form becomes blank awaiting your entry of the search criteria.

3 Type in the last name of the sales representative you are searching for (for example, **Estes**).

4 Click the **Find Next** button. Excel displays the first matching record. Continue clicking on the **Find Next** button until the record you want is displayed.

Task 5: Modifying a Record

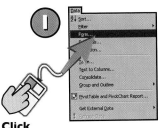

Click

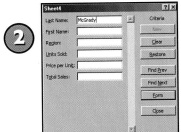

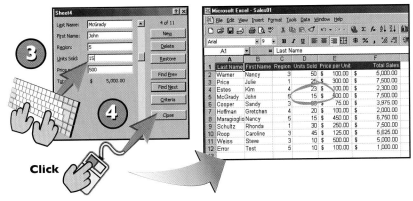

Click

Modifying a Data List Record

Maybe you entered in some records, but now you need to add some updates. Perhaps the **Units Sold** field has increased for one of your sales representatives. You would first need to find the record (using Task 4) and then modify the entry in the data list form.

1 Choose **Data**, **Form** to open the data form for the worksheet data list you created in Task 1 (unless you still have it open).

2 Find the record you want to modify using the steps in Task 4 to help you locate the record.

3 Type the edits to the field (for example, increase the **Units Sold** from **10** to **15**).

4 Click the **Close** button to accept the change and return to the worksheet data list.

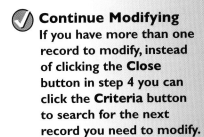

Continue Modifying
If you have more than one record to modify, instead of clicking the **Close** button in step 4 you can click the **Criteria** button to search for the next record you need to modify.

Task 6: Deleting Data Records

Removing a Record from the Data List

If a record is no longer valid, you can delete it. That row and all its data is removed from the worksheet. If you use the data form, you cannot undo the deletion. Be sure to check before you confirm the deletion.

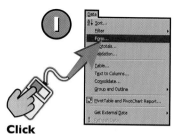

Click

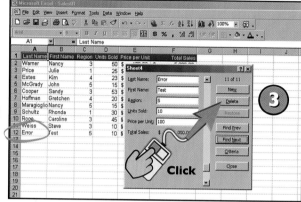

✓ **Delete in a Worksheet**
To delete a record in the worksheet, select the row and then choose **Edit, Delete.** The row and information are deleted from the worksheet.

✓ **Undo Deletion**
To undo a row deletion, use the **Undo** button on the Standard toolbar. You cannot undo a record deletion using the **Delete** button in the data form.

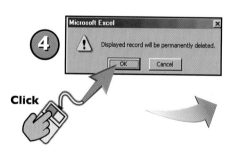

Click

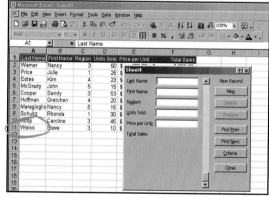

1 Choose **Data, Form** to open the data form for the worksheet data list you created in Task 1 (unless you still have it open).

2 Find the record you want to delete using the steps in Task 4 to help you locate the record.

3 Click the **Delete** button to permanently remove the record from the data list.

4 Click the **OK** button in the message box if you want to permanently delete the record from the data list; click the **Cancel** button if you don't want to delete the record.

Task 7: Sorting a Data List

Start Here

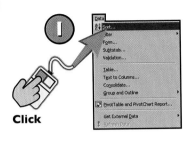
Click

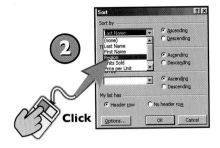
Click

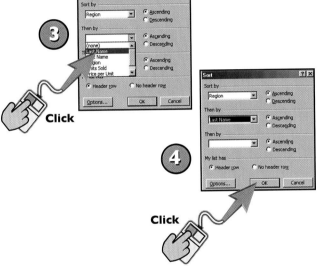
Click

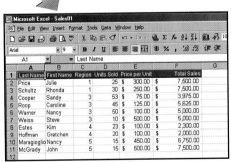
Click

Sorting the Records

It's easy to change the order of your database. In a sales representatives data list, for example, you may want to arrange the names alphabetically. You can sort on the Last Name field. As another possibility, you may want to sort your sales representatives by the region they work in. You could sort by the Region and Last Name fields.

① Choose **Data**, **Sort** to open the Sort dialog box.

② Click **Region** from the **Sort by** drop-down list **Ascending** for the first sort criteria.

③ Click **Last Name** from the **Then by** drop-down list **Ascending** for the second sort criteria.

④ Click the **OK** button and Excel sorts the entire data list.

Minimize the Sort

If you don't select the area of the data list that you want to sort, Excel sorts the entire list. You can, though, sort only on a particular number of records by first selecting the records in the data list and then following the steps in this task.

End Task

Task 8: Filtering a Data List

Displaying Filtered Records

In large data lists, you may not want to see each record. Instead, you may want to work with just a set of records—for example, all sales representatives in Region 3. When you want to work with a subset of records, you can filter the data. All the records remain in the database, but only those meeting the criteria you select are displayed.

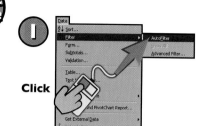

Click

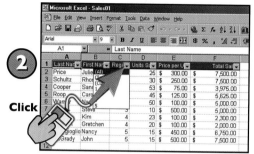

Click

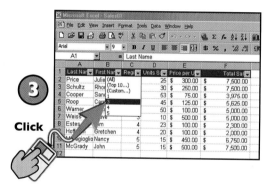

Click

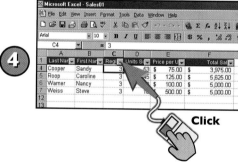

Click

✔ **Redisplay All Records**
To display all records again, you can choose **Data, Filter, Show All**. Or, you can click the arrow with the different filter color and select **All** from the drop-down list.

  Choose **Data**, **Filter**, **AutoFilter** to add drop-down arrows to each field header.

  Click the arrow next to the column you want to use for the filtering criteria (for example, **Region**).

  Select what records you want to match. You can select a particular value, Top 10, All, Custom, or a specific record type in that field (for example, **3**).

  Click in the data list. Excel is already displaying only those records that meet the selected criteria. You can tell the database has been filtered because the filter arrow is a different color.

Task 9: Removing an AutoFilter

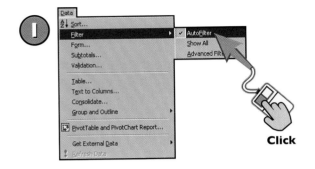

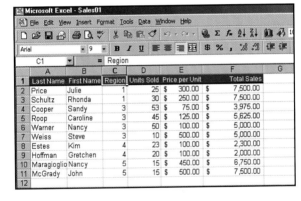

Turning AutoFilter Off

To avoid confusion, you will most likely want to turn the AutoFilter option off. This leaves the data list so that it is in its original format.

1 Choose **Data**, **Filter**, **AutoFilter**. The arrows disappear and the entire data list is again visible.

 Leave AutoFilter On
Another option to leaving your data list so that all records are visible is to leave the AutoFilter on, but deselect all the AutoFilter options you might have selected.

Task 10: Adding Record Subtotals

Summarizing Data in a List

Subtotals are an easy way to summarize data in a list. You might, for example, want to total all sales by a particular Region and then view a grand total. You may want to total sales by sales representative. If you have divided data into categories, you can sort and then subtotal on any field in the data list.

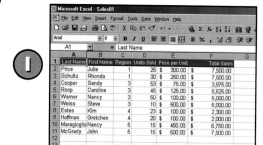

Click

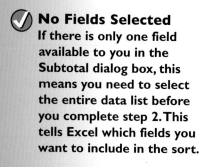

No Fields Selected

If there is only one field available to you in the Subtotal dialog box, this means you need to select the entire data list before you complete step 2. This tells Excel which fields you want to include in the sort.

1 Sort the data in the column you want to subtotal using the steps in Task 7 (for example, by **Region** and **Last Name**).

2 Choose **Data**, **Subtotals** to open the Subtotal dialog box.

3 Click **Region** from the **At each change in** drop-down list.

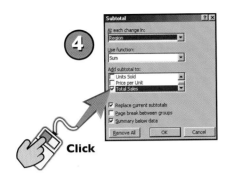

Click

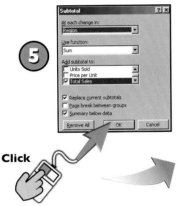

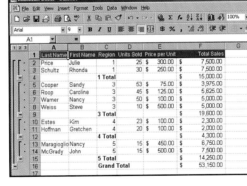

Click

④ Click the **Total Sales** option from the **Add subtotal to** list box. The default **Sum Use function** will calculate on the Total Sales field.

⑤ Click the **OK** button. Excel inserts a subtotal row for each time the selected field changes, performs the selected function on the column you asked to total, and adds a grand total at the end of the data list.

✅ **Multiple Calculations**
You can check more than one check box to have Excel calculate the function on each selected field.

✅ **Removing Subtotals**
To remove the subtotals, select the **Data, Subtotals** command. Click the Remove All button.

Printing Workbooks

In Excel you can print your worksheets by using a basic printing procedure, or you can enhance the printout with several print options.

Options for setting up the printed page include orientation, scaling, paper size, and page numbering. You can use these options to change how the worksheet is printed on the page (across or down). Another handy change is to scale the worksheet so that it fits on one (or two) pages.

Sheet options control what prints—gridlines, notes, row headings, and so on. You might want to make some changes. If you don't like the clutter of all the gridlines, for example, you can turn off gridlines. Another common change is to repeat column or row headings on a multipage worksheet. On worksheets that span two pages, the information on the second page might not make sense without proper headings.

Tasks

Task 1: Using Print Preview

Viewing Workbooks Before Printing

Workbooks with lots of data can generate large print jobs, possibly containing hundreds of pages. Waiting until all these pages are printed to verify that the information is printed correctly can cost a lot in both time and printing supplies. To help prevent printing mistakes, use Print Preview to ensure that all of the necessary elements appear on the pages being printed.

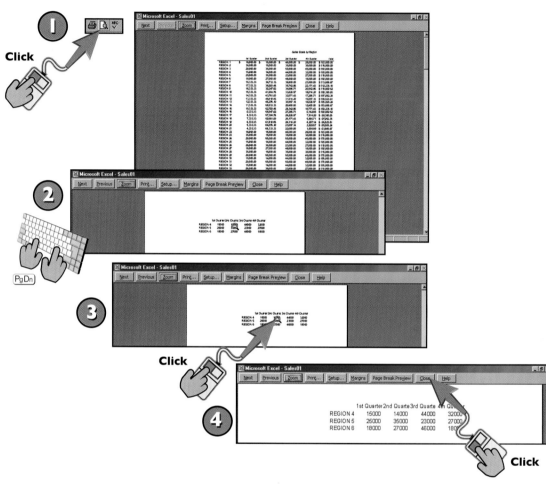

Click

Click

Click

✓ **Set Print Area**
If you don't want your printout (or print preview) to show the extra data that is off to the right or way down below your intended data, set the print area to exactly the data you want. See Task 2 for more information.

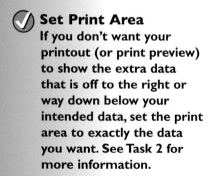

1 Click the **Print Preview** button on the Standard toolbar.

2 Press the **Page Down** key on the keyboard to scroll through the pages of your worksheet. Notice that the worksheet continues for multiple pages because there is data off to the right of the worksheet.

3 Click directly on the previewed worksheet when the mouse pointer becomes a magnifying glass; each click will toggle between zooming in to the data and zooming out.

4 Click the **Close** button to leave print preview and return to the worksheet.

End Task

Task 2: Setting the Print Area

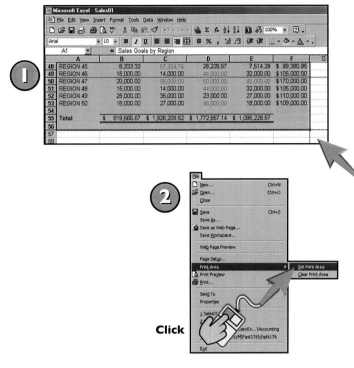

Click

Click

Choosing What to Print

Worksheets can cover a large number of rows and columns. Setting the print area enables you to specify exactly which rows and columns will print. If you don't have a print area set when you print, all cells that have any data in them will print. Sometimes this prints cells way off to the right or down the worksheet that you never intended to print.

1 Select the cells you want to print.

2 Choose **File**, **Print Area**, **Set Print Area**.

3 Click the **Print Preview** button on the Standard toolbar; now the print area only consists of two pages.

✓ **Print All on a Single Page**
Setting the print area does not cause all information to be printed on a single page. To do that, use the Scaling option in the Page Setup dialog box. See Task 7 for more information.

Task 3: Setting Margins

Changing Page and Column Widths

Margins affect where data is printed on a page. They also determine where headers and footers are printed. These might be changed to conform to company standards or to make room for a letterhead or logo on preprinted stationery. When in print preview, Excel allows you to alter your column widths the same as the margins.

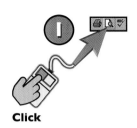

Click

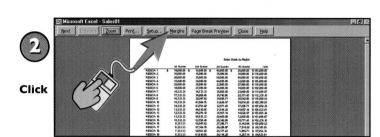

Click

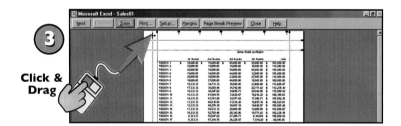

Click & Drag

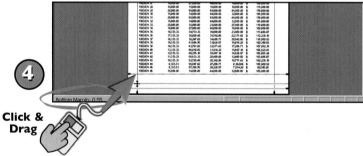

Click & Drag

✓ **Page Setup**

You also can alter your page margins without being in print preview. To do so, choose **File, Page Setup**, and click the ~~rg~~ins tab. Enter the ~~marg~~ins you want and click ~~O~~K button.

1 Click the **Print Preview** button on the Standard toolbar.

2 Click the **Margins** button on the Print Preview toolbar in the print preview window. The top, bottom, left, right, and header/footer margins appear as well as the column width indicators.

3 Click the **Left Margin**, drag it to decrease it to **.50** inches, and release the mouse button; the status bar will indicate the margin size as you drag it.

4 Click and drag the **Total** column indicator to a width of **17.00**, the **Footer Margin** to **.30** inches, and the **Bottom Margin** to **.55** inches.

Next Step

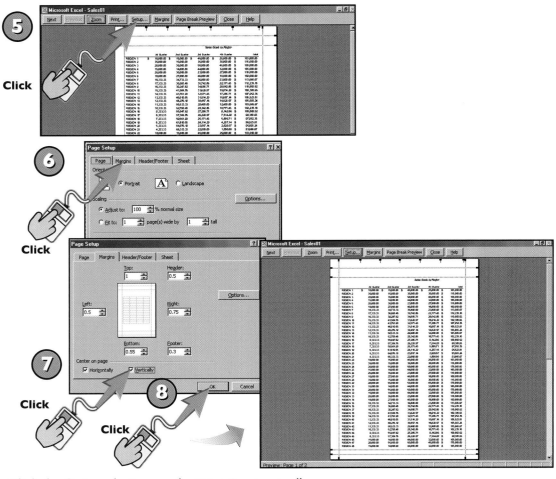

⑤ Click the **Setup** button on the Print Preview toolbar.

⑥ Click the **Margins** tab on the Page Setup dialog box.

⑦ Click to **Horizontally** and **Vertically Center on page**.

⑧ Click the **OK** button to accept the changes and see how your worksheet looks.

✔ Other Buttons
To view other pages in the worksheet, click the **Next** or **Previous** buttons on the Print Preview toolbar. To print the worksheet, click the **Print** button.

✔ Remove Margin Indicators
If you don't want to see the margin indicators in print preview, click the **Margins** button on the Print Preview toolbar again to toggle the margins off.

End Task

Task 4: Setting Page Orientation

Choosing Portrait or Landscape Print

You will find that depending on the data in your worksheet, it might be more appropriate to present your printed worksheet in one of two different orientation options. These options are vertically (portrait) or horizontally (landscape).

Click

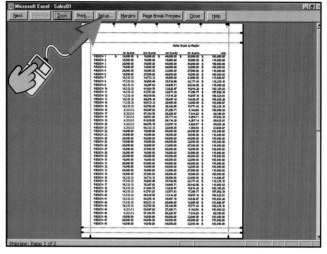

Click

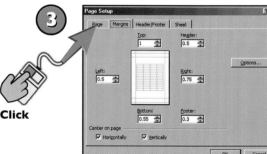

Click

✓ Margins
If you're using Print Preview and you decide you want to alter your margins, you can click the **Margins** button. The margin guides become visible. Click and drag any of the margin or column guides to see how you can alter your worksheet.

 Click the **Print Preview** button on the Standard toolbar.

 Click the **Setup** button on the Print Preview toolbar in the print preview window.

 Click the **Page** tab on the Page Setup dialog box.

Next Step

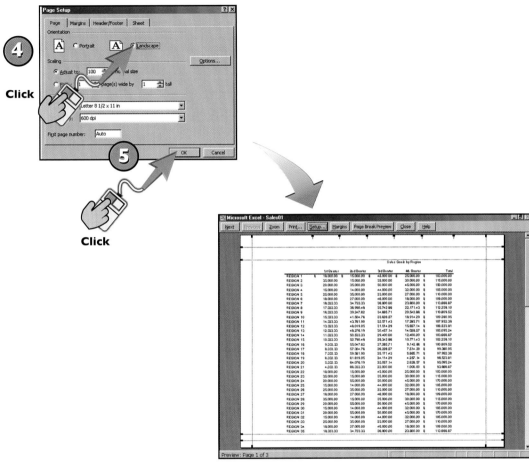

Click

Click

Remove Center Option
If you don't want your worksheet to be centered when in the landscape orientation, choose **Setup**, **Margins** tab, uncheck the **Horizontally** and **Vertically** options, and click the **OK** button to accept the changes.

④ Click the **Landscape Orientation** option.

⑤ Click the **OK** button to accept the changes and see how your worksheet looks.

Back to Portrait
You can easily switch your worksheet back to portrait orientation by following this task's steps and selecting the **Portrait Orientation** option instead.

Task 5: Inserting a Page Break

Force a Worksheet Break Point

Excel enters page breaks automatically, based on the page setup options you have selected (margins, scaling, and so on). If needed, you can force a page break. Suppose that your worksheet contains sales summary information for all regions in your company, and you want half of the regions to print on a separate page. You can enter page breaks.

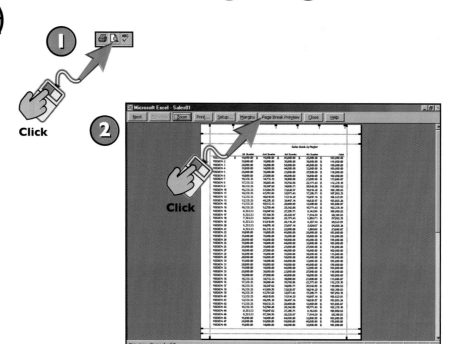

Start Here

Click

Click

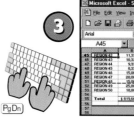

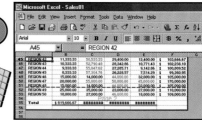

✓ View Page Break Preview

You don't have to be in the Print Preview window to get to the Page Break Preview window. Choosing View, Page Break Preview accomplishes the same task.

1 Click the **Print Preview** button on the Standard toolbar.

2 Click the **Page Break Preview** button on the Print Preview toolbar in the print preview window.

3 Press the **Page Down** key on the keyboard to see where the dotted line indicates the automatic page break.

Next Step

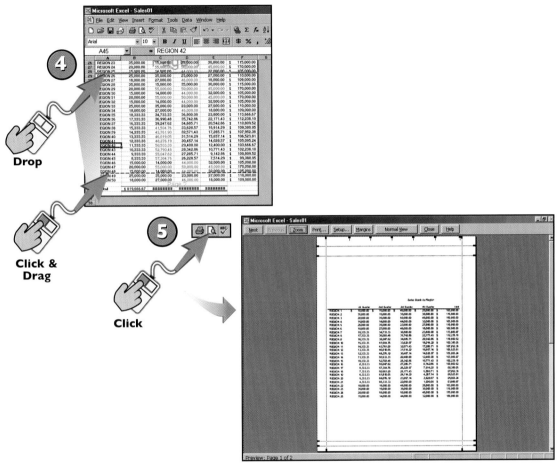

Drop

**Click &
Drag**

Click

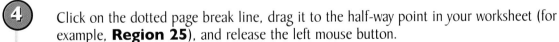

✓ **Scaling Breaks**
If you have your worksheet
scaled to fit on one page,
the page breaks won't
appear in page break
preview. See Task 7 for
more information on
scaling your worksheet
printouts.

(4) Click on the dotted page break line, drag it to the half-way point in your worksheet (for
example, **Region 25**), and release the left mouse button.

(5) Click the **Print Preview** button on the Standard toolbar to see how your worksheet
looks.

✓ **Removing Page Breaks**
To remove a page break,
select the cell immediately
to the right of the page
break, and then select the
**Insert, Remove Page
Break** command.

Task 6: Creating Repeating Titles

Repeating Rows and Columns

You might have noticed that when you have a worksheet that carries over to multiple pages, it is difficult to keep the column and/or row titles organized. A quick way to avoid this confusion is to assign particular titles to repeat on each page of the printed worksheet.

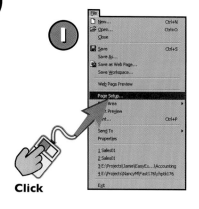

Click

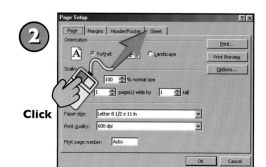

Click

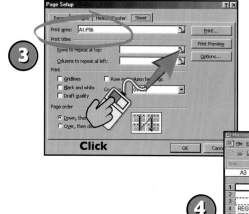

Click

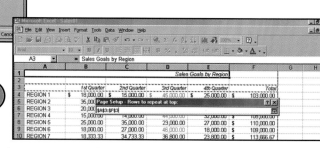

✓ **Repeat Titles in Print Preview**
You cannot assign repeating titles while you are in the Print Preview window, you must be in the worksheet view and select File, Page Setup.

① Choose **File**, **Page Setup** to open the Page Setup dialog box.

② Click the **Sheet** tab on the Page Setup dialog box.

③ Click the **Rows to repeat at top** selection box in the Print titles area. Notice that the Print area you selected in Task 2 is listed on this tab.

④ Select the column titles you want to repeat at the top of your printout.

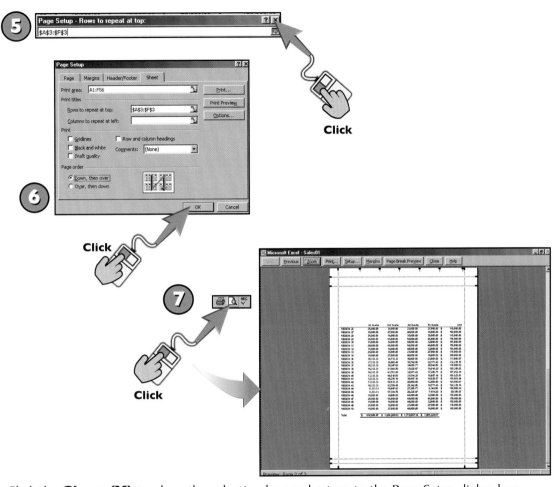

Click

Click

Click

(5) Click the **Close (X)** to close the selection box and return to the Page Setup dialog box.

(6) Click the **OK** button to accept your changes.

(7) Click the **Print Preview** button on the Standard toolbar and page through your document to see the repeated titles.

✓ **Columns to Repeat at Left**
You may want to repeat the columns at the left when you have numerous columns associated with a particular row header. For example, if you had regional sales information for each month in a separate column, you would probably need to repeat the column titles at the left to keep track of which region went with which month.

Task 7: Altering the Page Scale

Scaling a Worksheet

By default, Excel prints your worksheet at a scale of 100%. You can decrease this percentage if you want to fit more data on a page or larger if you want to fit less data on a page. In addition, you can have Excel fit your entire worksheet on one page. The only drawback to this is that if your worksheet is large, the data might become too tiny to read when scaled down so small.

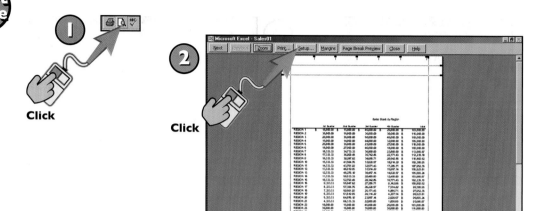

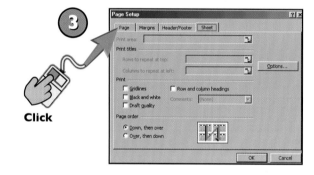

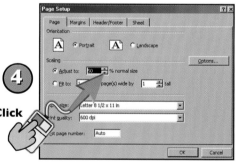

Click

⊘ Page Setup Option Button

If you click the Option button from anywhere on the Page Setup dialog box, you can choose different types of letter sizes. This is convenient if you need to print your worksheet on legal-sized paper. The scaling setting automatically adjusts to the different sized paper.

1 Click the **Print Preview** button on the Standard toolbar.

2 Click the **Setup** button on the Print Preview toolbar in the print preview window.

3 Click the **Page** tab on the Page Setup dialog box.

4 Click the **Adjust to** spin box so that it is **50% normal size**.

Next
Step

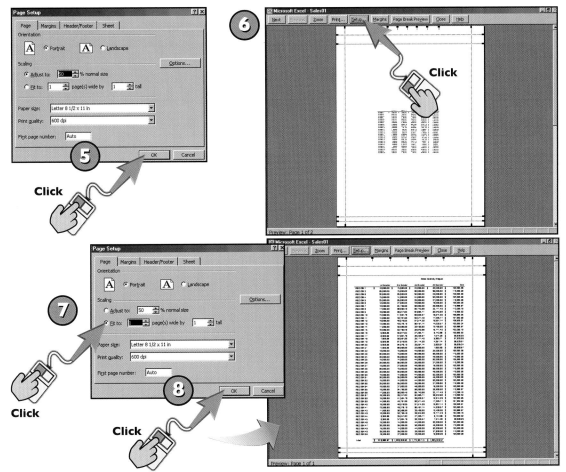

Click

Click

Click

Click

Fit to Percentage
If you return to the Page tab of the Page Setup dialog box after you have selected the worksheet to be fitted to 1 page wide by 1 tall, you will notice that the percentage auto-matically adjusts to whatever Excel had to make fit one page.

Returning to Default Scale
When you want to return the preview of your work-sheet to the default scale, select the **Adjust to** option and type 100 into the % normal size spin box.

⑤ Click the **OK** button to preview your worksheet.

⑥ Click the **Setup** button again to return to the Page tab.

⑦ Click the **Fit to** option so that it is **1 page wide by 1 tall**.

⑧ Click the **OK** button to see how your worksheet previews.

Adding Information to the Header and Footer

Headers and footers appear at the top and bottom of printed pages of Excel worksheets. Headers and footers can display the filename, date and time printed, worksheet name, page number, and more. Excel offers many standard headers and footers to choose from, or you can create custom headers and footers. This task shows you an example of each.

Task 8: Creating Headers and Footers

Click

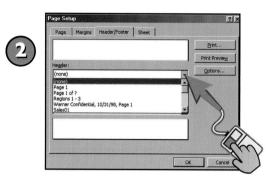

Click

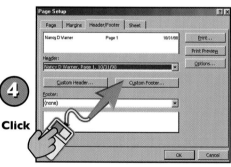

Click

Click

✓ **Print Preview Header and Footer**
You can alter your header and footer while in the Print Preview window by selecting the **Setup** button on the Print Preview toolbar and clicking the **Header/Footer** tab.

① Choose **View**, **Header and Footer** to open the Page Setup dialog box to the Header/Footer tab.

② Click the **Header** drop-down list box to see the various header options.

③ Click the option you want (for example, **name**, **page number**, **date**) to be in the left, center, and right section of the header.

④ Click the **Custom Footer** button if you want to create your own footer; or click the Footer drop-down list box and select from the options.

Next Step

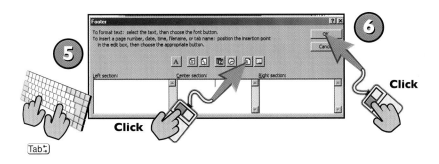

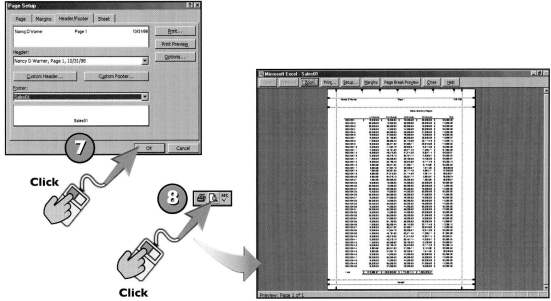

Click

Page Number and Count

Add page numbers and the total page count to the header or footer to read, for example, "Page 2 of 7." Adding page numbers and count makes it easier to reorganize papers if they are dropped and alerts someone if some of the pages are missing.

(5) Press the **Tab** key to move to the Center section and click the **Filename** button to insert the workbook filename field into the Footer section.

(6) Click the **OK** button to accept the Footer text.

(7) Click the **OK** button to accept the Header and Footer text.

(8) Click the **Print Preview** button on the Standard toolbar to see how your worksheet previews.

No Header or Footer

If you don't want to use a header or footer, display the Header/Footer tab, click the **Header or Footer** drop-down list and select **(none)**.

End Task

Getting Hard Copy

Printing a workbook is quite simple, but setting the options for printing a workbook can be complex. The number of options that must be set before printing a workbook depends on the amount of data stored in the workbook, how it is arranged, how much of it needs to be printed, and how you want the printout to look.

Task 9: Printing Workbooks and Worksheets

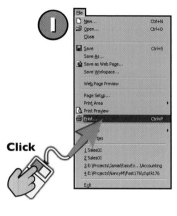

Click

Click

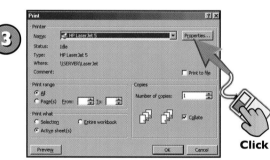

Click

✓ **Default Print**
To print the worksheet using the default settings in the Print dialog box, click the **Print** button. You also can press **Ctrl+P** and click the **OK** button in the Print dialog box.

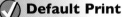 Choose **File**, **Print** to open the Print dialog box.

 Click the **Printer Name** drop-down list to choose an available printer or fax option.

 Click the **Properties** button to choose different paper sizes, graphics options, font options, and printer's details.

Next
Step

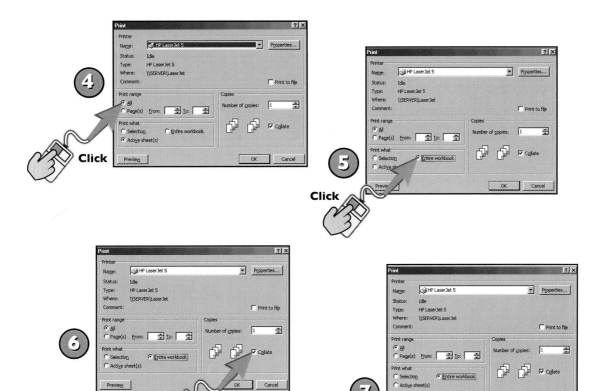

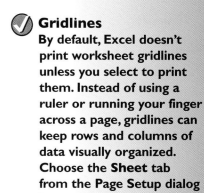

Gridlines

By default, Excel doesn't print worksheet gridlines unless you select to print them. Instead of using a ruler or running your finger across a page, gridlines can keep rows and columns of data visually organized. Choose the **Sheet** tab from the **Page Setup** dialog box and select the **Gridlines** option.

Page Order

If you are working with a large worksheet, you can specify the page order that your worksheet is printed. The default is down your worksheet then over; you can also select over, then down. This is convenient if you have numerous columns that you want printed according to a specific row header.

Cancel Print

Click the **Cancel** button on the Print dialog box to cancel the print. In addition, if you already sent the workbook to the printer, click the **Cancel** button on the Printing message box.

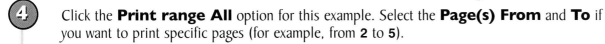

4   Click the **Print range All** option for this example. Select the **Page(s) From** and **To** if you want to print specific pages (for example, from **2** to **5**).

5   Click the **Print what Entire workbook** option to print all the worksheets in your workbook; **Selection** prints specific cells; **Active Sheet(s)** prints the sheet you are currently in.

6   Select the **Number of copies: 1** (default) and to **Collate** (print in page order).

7   Click the **OK** button to send your printout to the printer. Click the **Preview** button to preview your printout (then choose the **Print** button from the Print Preview window toolbar).

Advanced Excel and Web Features

Throughout this book you have learned about features in Excel that help you accomplish tasks and make your work easier. This final part is going to take you a step further with Excel so that you can copy and **link** data with other documents, **import** and **export** data, and even automate repetitive tasks with **macros**.

There are numerous Excel 2000 features that can make working with the Internet and the Web easier and more convenient. You will learn how to save an Excel workbook as a Web page and open it up in a **browser**. You can add **URLs** and all kinds of **hyperlinks** to your worksheets. In addition, you can edit and remove hyperlinks using the new Hyperlink dialog box. You can even add email hyperlinks, send your worksheets as email messages, or send them as a fax.

To utilize the Web and Internet features in Excel 2000, you need to have access to the Internet. You might have an account with an online service (for example, America Online), with a local Internet Service Provider (ISP), or in a corporate setting where you have to log into the network to gain Internet access. You need to connect to the Internet to perform the tasks in this part.

Tasks

Task 1: Copying and Linking to Office Documents

Copying and Linking Workbooks with Documents

Up until now you have learned about the many ways you can copy and paste items in your workbooks. This task is going to take you a step further by showing you how to copy and link your workbooks to other Office documents—Word documents for example. Copying and linking are two different things and this task shows you the difference.

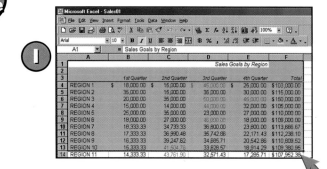

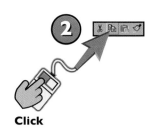

Click

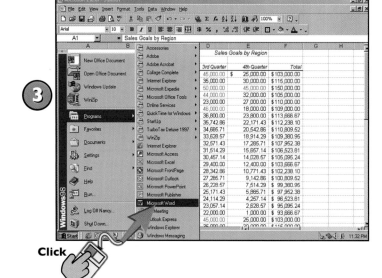

Click

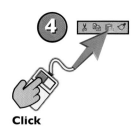

Click

✓ Starting Applications
You can start other applications just as easily as you started the Excel application. Click on the **Start** button and click on the application in the **Programs** menu. Refer to Part 1, Task 1 on starting Excel.

1. Select the Excel worksheet cells that you want to copy or link to a Word document.

2. Click the **Copy** button on the Standard toolbar.

3. Open up a new, blank Microsoft Word document.

4. Click the **Paste** button on the Word Standard toolbar; the cells are copied (*not linked*) in your Word document.

Next Step

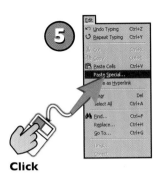

Click

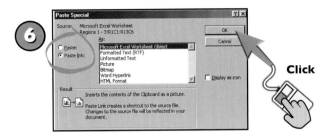

Click

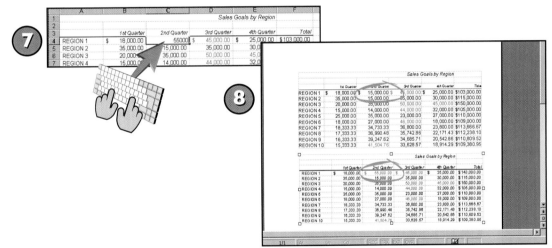

✓ **Paste as Hyperlink**
Besides pasting cells as a link to another document, you can paste cells as a hyperlink. This will allow you to click on the items in the pasted area and immediately be hyperlinked to your original workbook that contains the cells. Choose **Edit, Paste Hyperlink** in the document you are pasting into.

✓ **Switching Applications**
You can switch between applications just as easily as you can switch between workbooks. Click on the taskbar button to switch between all open items. Refer to Part 2, Task 6 for switching between workbooks.

5 Choose **Edit, Paste Special**.

6 Select the **Paste link** option **As Microsoft Excel Worksheet Object** and click the **OK** button; the cells are linked (*not copied*) in your Word document.

7 Switch back to your Excel workbook and type a change into the contents of one of the cells that you copied (for example, **C4** = **55000**).

8 Switch to the Word document and see that the cell content change was updated on the linked cells, but not the copied cells.

End Task

Automating Repetitive Tasks with Macros

You can create a macro that accomplishes just about any task. You don't even have to know anything about programming. With the macro recording option, you can record your actions and these actions are performed for you when you run the macro. For example, if you create a lot of quarterly workbooks, you might create a macro that opens up a new blank workbook for you and adds the appropriate column heading information automatically.

 Pause Recording
When you click the **Pause Recording** button, the macro recording procedure is paused. When you click the **Stop Recording** button, the macro stops for good.

Task 2: Creating and Running Macros

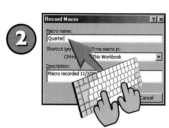

Click

Click

Click

---

1 Choose **Tools**, **Macro**, **Record New Macro**.

2 Type a name for the macro. Name it something you can easily remember that has to do with what the macro will accomplish (for example, **Quarter**).

3 Click the **OK** button. The Macro toolbar appears with the Stop Recording and Pause Recording buttons visible.

4 Click the **New** button on the Standard toolbar to create a new workbook.

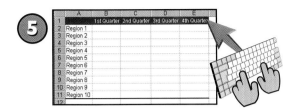

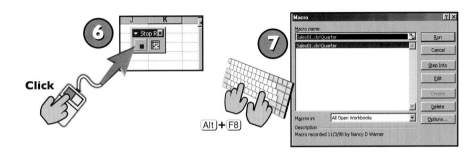

Click

Alt + F8

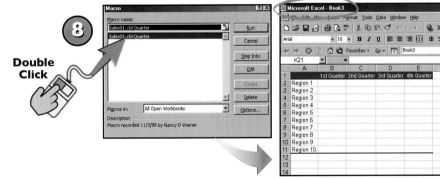

**Double
Click**

Everything Records
Keep in mind that when the macro is recording, everything you do is recorded. For example, if you page down through a worksheet, that will happen when you run the macro later. Try to use the Pause Recording button if you aren't sure of something you want to record.

Adding Macros to your Toolbars
You learned how to add buttons to your toolbars in Part 1, Task 7 "Working with Toolbars." Macros are also items that you can add to your toolbars to make it easy to launch them. For example, follow along the steps of adding a button to your toolbar, but choose Macros from the Categories list. Then choose the specific macro in the Commands list. It is as simple as that.

---

5 Type in the information you want to appear when you run the macro; you can add whatever you want and any formatting you like.

6 Click the **Stop Recording** button.

7 Press the **Alt+F8** keys to open the Macros dialog box.

8 Double-click on the Macro name and the macro will run (opening a new workbook and inserting the text you typed).

Task 3: Exporting Data

Saving Data for Use in Another Application

You might find that after you have been saving information in your workbook for a while, you want to use the data in another application. For example, you might want to upload the Regional Sales data to a database for more extensive reporting tools (or use it in a Word mail merge. This task will show you how to save your Excel worksheet data in a tab delimited format that other applications can use and view what that data looks like.

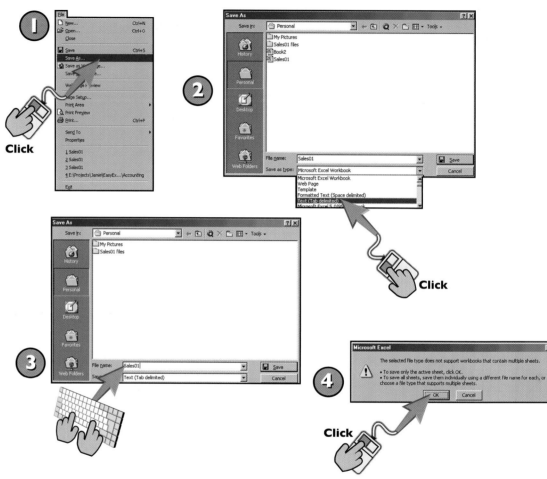

Click

Click

Click

✓ **Exporting Formatting**
When you create a tab delimited file for use in other applications, the *data* in the cells is the important information you are saving to export. The formatting in the cells (bold, blue, italic, and so on) is not saved because it is not necessary to the data.

① Choose **File**, **Save As** to open the Save As dialog box.

② Select the **Save as type** drop-down list box option of **Text (Tab delimited)**.

③ Type a **File name** (or keep the current workbook name) and press the **Enter** key.

④ Click the **OK** button in the message box to save only the workbook's active sheet. You must save worksheets individually for them to be tab delimited and saved.

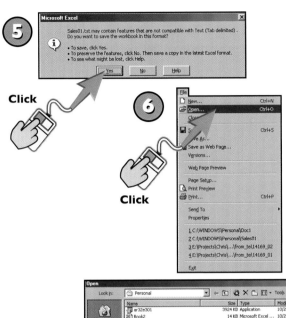

Click

Click

Click

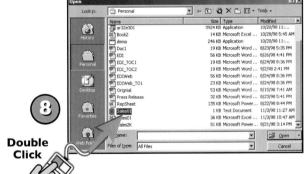

Double
Click

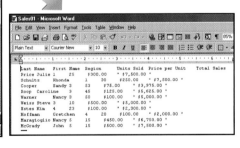

Starting Applications
You can start other applications just as easily as you started the Excel application. Simply click the **Start** button and click the application in the **Programs** menu. Refer to Part 1, Task 1 on starting Excel.

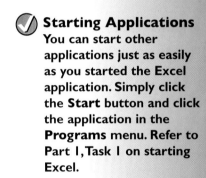

Exiting Excel
You can exit Excel by choosing **File, Exit** or clicking the **Close (X)** button in the application window. Refer to Part 1, Task 13 for more information on exiting Excel.

5 Click the **Yes** button so that it is understood that some of the worksheet and cell formatting might not be saved when you save the worksheet.

6 Exit Microsoft Excel and start Microsoft Word; choose **File, Open** to open the Microsoft Word Open dialog box.

7 Select **All Files** from the **Files of type** drop-down list box.

8 Double-click on the filename you just saved in step 3 to see what the tab delimited file looks like.

End Task

Task 4: Importing Data

Using Data from Another Application

This task is similar to the previous task in that to import data into Excel it must be in a format that Excel will accept (for example, a tab delimited text file). The example in this task uses the same file you just exported in Task 3 to import in this task.

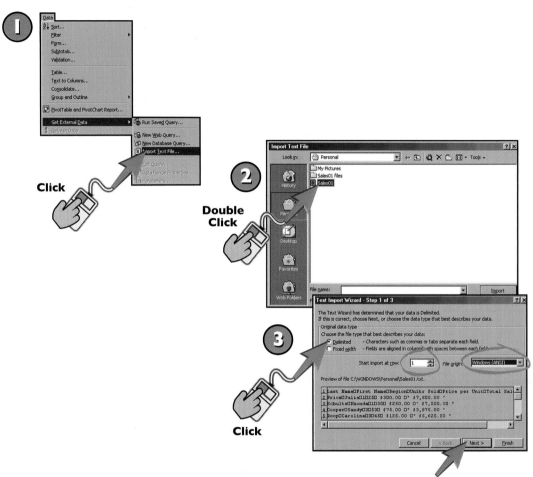

✓ Alternate File Locations

If necessary, click the **Look In** drop-down arrow and select the folder from the list. To move up a folder level, click the **Up One Level** button on the toolbar. If you double-click a subfolder, its contents appear in the list of files and folders.

1 Choose **Data**, **Get External Data**, **Import Text File** to open the Import Text File dialog box.

2 Double-click the text file you want to import and the Text Import Wizard dialog box opens.

3 Click the **Delimited** file type, because it describes the data in the file you are importing, the **Start import at row 1**, because you want the entire file, and the **File origin** of **Windows (ANSI)**, because it originated on a Windows operating system platform. Then, click the **Next** button to continue.

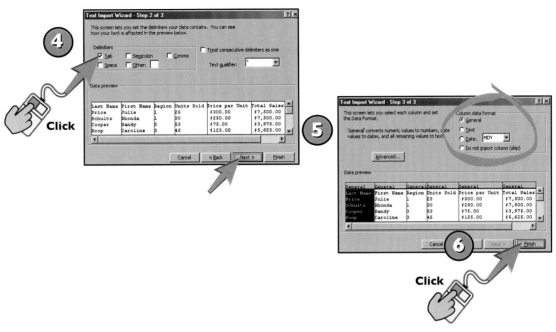

Click

Click

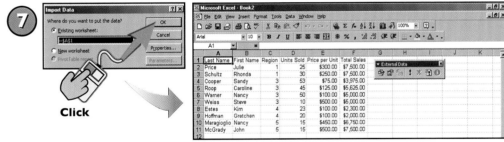

Click

④ Click the **Tab Delimiters** with the **Text qualifier** of " and click the **Next** button to continue.

⑤ Select the **Column data format** for your imported data to tell Excel whether a column of data is of the **General**, **Text**, or **Date** format; or, whether to import a particular column.

⑥ Click the **Finish** button because you want to import all the data in the **General** format.

⑦ Click the **OK** button in the Import Data dialog box to place the data in the existing worksheet beginning with cell **A1**.

End Task

✅ **Delimiters and Qualifiers**
Delimiters can be tab, semicolon, comma, space, or other types. These are the items that separate the data from other data. Qualifiers can be double, single, or no quotes. These are the items that qualify data as text.

✅ **External Data Toolbar**
The External Data toolbar opens automatically when you import data in this fashion. You can use the buttons on the toolbar or close the toolbar and work with the new data in your worksheet.

Creating a Worksheet Web Page

To use your Excel workbook as a Web page, you need to save it as the correct file format. Excel 2000 now has the capability to save your files in HTML format and allow you to open your workbooks back up in Excel and use the available Excel features.

✓ **Workbook Versus Worksheet**
Instead of saving the default entire workbook, you can select the option **Selection: Sheet** to save only the active worksheet as a Web page.

✓ **Other Office Applications**
Saving as a Web page is just as simple in the other applications in Office 2000. Follow the same procedure when using Word 2000 and PowerPoint 2000.

Task 5: Saving a Worksheet As a Web Page

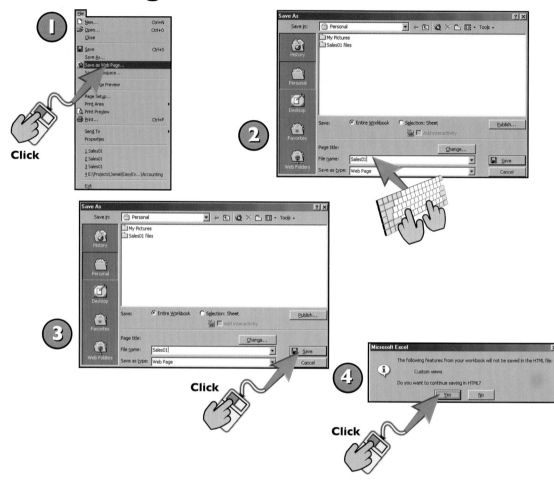

1 Choose **File**, **Save as Web Page** to open the Save As dialog box.

2 Type in the **File name** you would like the Web workbook saved as (for example, **Sales01**).

3 Click the **Save** button and the workbook saves with the filename you assigned in the title bar.

4 Click the **Yes** button to accept that custom views will be the only element not saved in an HTML file.

Task 6: Using Web Page Preview

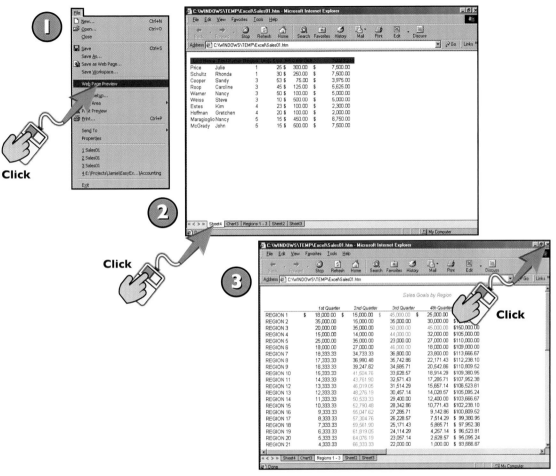

Click

Click

Click

Viewing Your Worksheet as a Web Page

Now that you have created a Web page you want to see what the workbook will look like to everyone else viewing your Web workbook. You can view your workbooks in Web Page Preview even before you have saved the file. This makes it easy to see exactly how the page will look.

✓ **Browser Buttons and Links**
Notice that the Web browser acts just like it is displaying an active Web page. The workbook name is in the menu bar and the Explorer bar buttons are active.

✓ **Other Office Applications**
Previewing a Web page is just as simple in the other applications in Office 2000. Follow the same procedure when using Word 2000 and PowerPoint 2000.

1 Choose **File**, **Web Page Preview** to view your workbook in your default Web browser.

2 Click the tabs at the bottom of the browser window to move through the workbook worksheets.

3 Click the **Close** (×) button to close the browser and return to your workbook in Excel.

Adding Hyperlinks to Worksheets

A URL (Uniform Resource Locator) is a link to an addressable location on the Internet. Excel 2000 lets you type URLs into your worksheets and automatically establishes a link. You will notice this link is a different color and underlined. This is called to a hyperlink.

✓ **Nonautomatic Hyperlinks**

If you type a URL into your worksheet and Excel 2000 doesn't recognize it automatically as a hyperlink, see Task 9, "Inserting Web Hyperlinks" to make it one.

✓ **Remove Hyperlinks**

If you are typing a hyperlink into a worksheet as an example and don't want it to be an active link, see Task 12 "Removing a Hyperlink."

Task 7: Typing a URL into a Worksheet

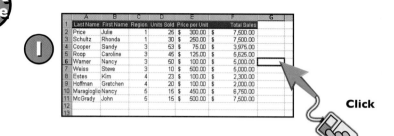

Click

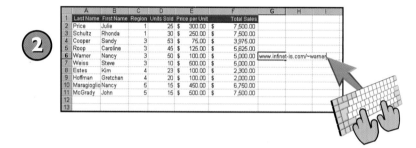

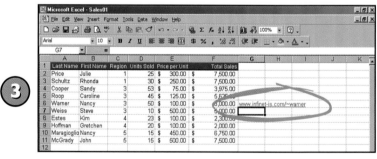

 Click the mouse pointer in the worksheet where you want to add the URL.

 Type the URL into your worksheet (for example, **www.infinet-is.com/~warner**).

 Press the **Enter** key; the address automatically becomes a hyperlink.

Task 8: Clicking a URL in a Worksheet

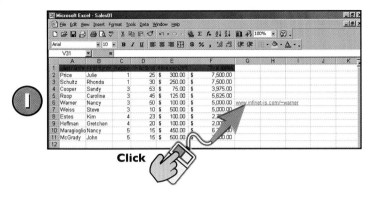

Click

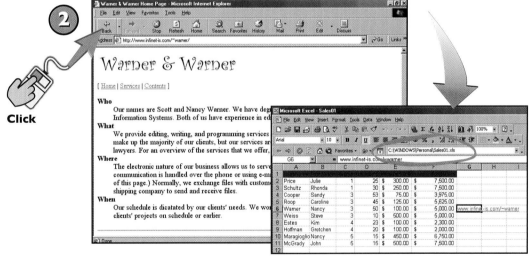

Click

Worksheet Links to the Web

If a hyperlink is clicked on in a worksheet, you will immediately be taken to the URL address in your application (if you are connected to the Internet) in read-only mode. Any links you click will take you to the specific Web site with your default Web browser.

✓ **Return to Your Workbook**

If you have finished browsing the Web, you can click the **X** button to close the Web browser or the Back button until you return to your Excel workbook. In addition, you could also click the workbook in the Windows taskbar to make it the active workbook.

① Click the **URL hyperlink** to link to the Web page in Excel.

② Click the **Back** button on the Web toolbar to move back to your original document. Notice that Excel's Web toolbar is now visible with the current Web document name in the Address drop-down list box.

End Task

Task 9: Inserting Web Hyperlinks

Adding Web Links to Your Worksheets

If you cannot remember the name of the hyperlink you want to add to your worksheet, you can use the **Insert Hyperlink** button on the Standard toolbar to help you out. From the Insert Hyperlink dialog box you can browse Web pages or use recent links to locate and add the correct address.

✓ Inserted Link
If the link you want to add to your worksheet isn't listed in the links list box, type the Web page name directly into the Insert Hyperlink dialog box.

✓ Graphics
In addition to making text into a hyperlink, you can click any other object and create a link. For example, you could make a piece of clip art, a chart, or a worksheet cell into a hyperlink.

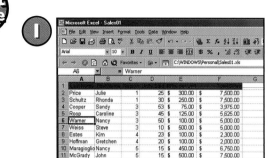

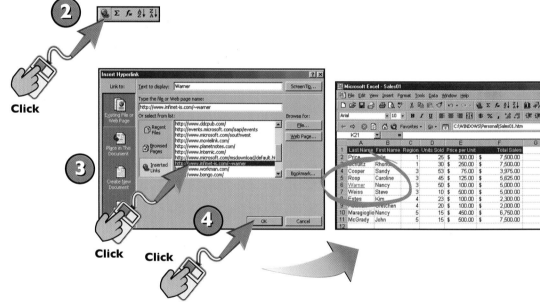

Click

Click   **Click**

1. Select the cell text that you want to make into a hyperlink.

2. Click the **Insert Hyperlink** button on the Standard toolbar to open the Insert Hyperlink dialog box.

3. Click an **Inserted Link** from the list box (for example, `www.infinet-is.com/~warner`).

4. Click the **OK** button to accept the link. Notice that the text now looks like a hyperlink.

End Task

Task 10: Inserting Office Document Hyperlinks

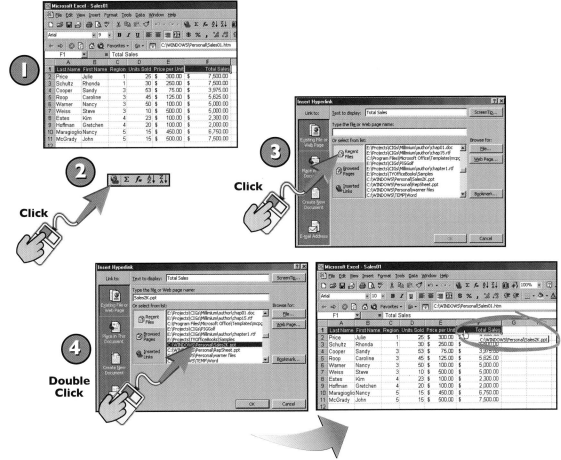

Click

Click

Double Click

Adding Document Links to Your Worksheets

Many times when creating an elaborate worksheet you will want to add a link that takes you or the reader to some other pertinent file. For example, you could add a monthly report presentation link to your sales worksheet so the report updates automatically.

✓ Email Hyperlinks

Sometimes you will be creating a document and want to add your email address for the reader to access immediately. For example, you create a report for your customers, but want them to email you as soon as they read the report, to let you know their thoughts. You can set up an email link in the document for them to do so immediately, without having to leave the document to go to their email application.

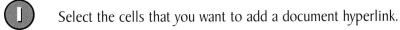

1. Select the cells that you want to add a document hyperlink.

2. Click the **Insert Hyperlink** button on the Standard toolbar to open the Insert Hyperlink dialog box.

3. Click the **Recent Files** button to see files on which you recently worked.

4. Double-click an **Inserted Link** from the list box. Move the mouse pointer over the new hyperlink.

Task 11: Editing a Hyperlink

Altering a Hyperlink

People aren't perfect, so you will invariably type in an incorrect hyperlink and need to edit it. In addition, some Web page addresses change frequently; you will need to update your hyperlinks to those pages.

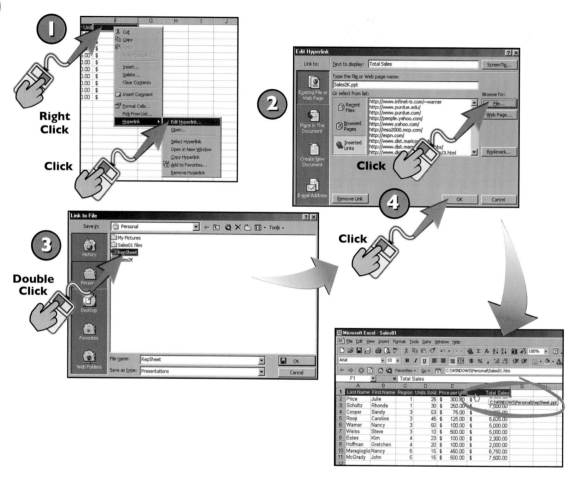

Start Here

Right Click

Click

Double Click

Click

Click

✓ Remove Links

Not only can you update a hyperlink in the Edit Hyperlink dialog box, you can remove the hyperlink if you decide to. Click the Remove Link button and click the **OK** button to close the Edit Hyperlink dialog box.

1 Right-click a hyperlink and choose **Hyperlink**, **Edit Hyperlink** to open the Edit Hyperlink dialog box.

2 Click the **File** button to select a different link.

3 Double-click the item you want to link to.

4 Click the **OK** button to accept the edits in the Edit Hyperlink dialog box. Move the mouse pointer over the hyperlink.

End Task

Task 12: Removing a Hyperlink

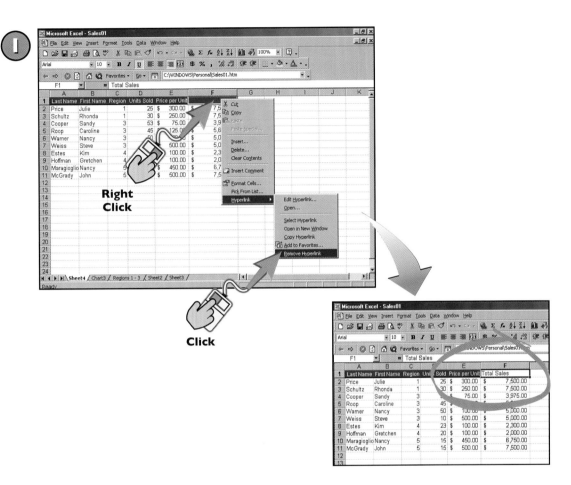

Right Click

Click

Deleting a Hyperlink

If you decide you no longer want a particular hyperlink in your worksheet, you can remove it. **Another reason you might want to remove a hyperlink is because maybe you didn't really intend for the worksheet to contain a hyperlink. Perhaps you were just referring to a particular Web page in a report, but didn't want people to use a link to it.**

Right-click a hyperlink and choose **Hyperlink**, **Remove Hyperlink** to delete the hyperlink. Notice that when you do this, it actually removes the cell's original formatting.

 Using the Undo

If you remove a hyperlink and decide you want it back in your worksheet, you can use the Undo button on the Standard toolbar and the hyperlink will be restored.

Task 13: Sending a Workbook As an Email

Emailing Workbooks

This feature in Excel is now a button on the Standard toolbar. You will find this feature fun to use if you want to get feedback on a report you are working on with a colleague in a different location.

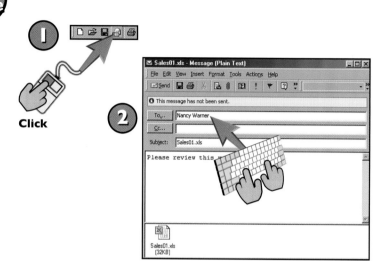

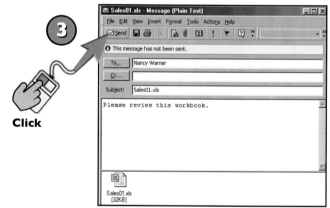

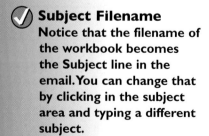

✓ **Subject Filename**

Notice that the filename of the workbook becomes the Subject line in the email. You can change that by clicking in the subject area and typing a different subject.

① Click the **E-mail** button on the Standard toolbar.

② Type the recipient name in the **To** area (try sending it to yourself) and any information you want in the body of the email message.

③ Click the **Send** button to mail the workbook and check the messages in your email client.

End Task

Task 14: Sending a Workbook As a Fax

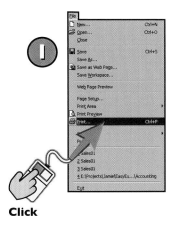

Click

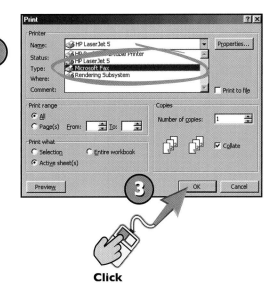

Click

Faxing Workbooks

Faxing a workbook is as easy as printing your workbook. You choose the fax option when selecting a printer and choose the other printing options just like you would if you were sending your workbook to a printer. Keep in mind that you must have fax software installed on your computer and a phone line you can dial out on.

Choose **File**, **Print** to open the Print dialog box.

Select **Microsoft Fax** from the **Printer Name** drop-down list box.

Click the **OK** button to send the fax. Depending on your fax software you will be asked to enter the phone number you want to fax to and if you want to create a fax cover letter.

Fax Modem Problems
If you encounter problems while you are faxing, you can use Excel help to troubleshoot potential problems with your modem or fax software.

Absolute cell reference   An entry in a formula that does not change when the formula is copied to a new cell. In certain formulas, you might want an entry to always refer to one specific cell value.

Active cell   The cell currently selected in an Excel worksheet.

Active worksheet   The worksheet currently selected in an Excel workbook.

Alignment   The way text lines up against the margins of a page. For example, justified text lines up evenly with both the left and right margins.

ANSI   American National Standards Institute. An organization that develops standards for computers.

Application   A program that is used on your computer.

Arguments   Words, phrases, or numbers you enter in a statement to modify the formula or function operation. For example, SUM.

Arrows   Items that can be clicked on in scrollbars to move throughout a workbook.

AutoFill   A feature in Excel that will automatically fill a series of information. For example, if you type January, February and select continuous empty cells, Excel will automatically fill them with the next logical option (March).

AutoText   A feature that automatically corrects mistyped text. You can also use AutoText to invent a string of characters that automatically corrects itself to a word or phrase. For example, Word comes with AutoText that automatically corrects "teh" to "the."

Axes   See *Category axis* and *Value axis*.

Browser   A tool that lets you view documents on the Internet.

Bullet   An object, such as a circle or square, used to set off items in a list.

Category axis   This is the y-axis on a chart.

Cell   An area in an Excel worksheet or a Word table that holds a specific piece of information.

Chart   A graphic representation of a selection of Excel workbook cell data.

Chart area   This is the area in a chart that contains information about the data that is being graphed.

Clip Gallery   A collection of clip art, pictures, sound files, and video clips you can use to spruce up Office documents.

Clipboard   Information that is cut or copied resides in this location in the Windows operating system. New to Windows 98 and Office 2000 is the capability to place as many as 12 items on the Clipboard and use any of them you want at any time.

Column   (1) In a table, a vertical set of cells. (2) In a document, the arrangement of text and graphics vertically so the document looks like a newspaper.

Conditional statement   A function that returns different results depending on whether a specified condition is true or false.

Context menu   See *Shortcut menu*.

Cursor   The location where you last entered text. This is a flashing bar in some applications.

Data   The information you work with in an Excel spreadsheet, including text, numbers, and graphics images.

Data label   This is a label for a data series in a chart.

Data range   This is the range for a data series in a chart.

Data table   This is a table in a chart that lists the data being graphed.

Data validation   This is the process of making sure that data is accurately entered into a form for a data list.

Datasheet   A grid of columns and rows that enables you to enter numerical data into a chart.

Dependents   These are cell references that depend on a formula or function.

Dialog box   Any of the information boxes that appear during the installation or use of an application and require input from the user.

Docked toolbar   Any toolbar that is attached to one of the four sides of an application window.

Document window   This is the window that controls the individual documents within an application window.

Drag-and-drop   To move an object (an icon, a selection of text, a cell in an Excel worksheet, and so on) by selecting it, dragging it to another location, and then releasing the mouse button.

Drop-down list   A list of choices presented when you click the arrow to the right of a field in a dialog box.

Embedded object   This is when a source and destination file aren't linked,

which means that when one object is updated, the other is not. The embedded object is physically included in the document to which it belongs.

Equation   This is a formula or function used in Excel to perform calculations.

Export   To put the data in your application into a format that other applications can use.

External data   Data from a location other than the application you are currently working in.

Field   This is a place where you enter data in a data list or a data element on a form.

File   Information you enter in your computer and save for future use, such as a document or a workbook.

Filter   A method in Excel for controlling which records are extracted from the database and displayed in the worksheet.

Floating toolbar   A toolbar that is not anchored to the edge of the window, but instead displays in the document window for easy access. In addition, you can drag a floating toolbar out to your Windows desktop.

Font   The typeface, type size, and type attributes of text or numbers.

Footer   Text or graphics that appear at the bottom of the page of a document or worksheet.

Form   This is a window you can create in Excel that you can use to add data list records.

Format   To change the appearance of text or numbers.

Format Painter   This enables you to quickly format data exactly like other data.

Formatting   Applying attributes to text and data to change the appearance of information.

Formula bar   This is where Excel calculation and formatting elements are listed.

Formula palette   This is a list of formulas that are usable in Excel.

Formulas   In Excel, a means for calculating a value based on the values in other cells of the workbook.

Function   A built-in formula that automatically performs calculations in Excel.

Graphics   Images that come in all shapes and sizes. Typical graphics include clip art images, drawings, photographs, scanned images, and signature files.

Grid   This is the relation or rows to columns.

Gridlines   Lines that separate the cells in a printed workbook.

Handles   The small, black squares around a selected object. You use these squares to drag, size, or scale the object.

Header   Text or graphics that appear at the top of every page of a document or workbook.

Highlight   A band of color you can add to text by using the Highlight tool on the Word toolbar. In addition, when you select text to format or move, for example, you are selecting or "highlighting" the text.

Hyperlinks   Text formatted so that clicking it "jumps" you to another, related location.

I-beam   The shape of the mouse pointer when you move over a screen area in which you can edit text.

Import   To bring data into an application from another application.

Indent   An amount of space that an object, usually text, is moved away from the left margin.

Insert mode   This is when the new text you enter moves the text that was

previously in the same location over to the right.

Insertion point   The blinking vertical bar that shows where text will appear when you type. The insertion point is sometimes called a cursor.

Internet   A system of linked computer networks that facilitate data communication services such as remote login, file transfer, electronic mail, and newsgroups.

Justify   Aligning text so it fills the area between the left and right margins.

Landscape   This is the wide view of a printout.

Legend   This is a way of understanding the elements in a chart and what they represent.

Link   This is a representation between a linked object and a source object. If one of the objects are altered, the other is altered as well.

Macro   A method of automating common tasks you perform in applications such as Word or Excel. You can record keystrokes and mouse clicks so they can be played back automatically.

Margins   The space around the top, bottom, left, and right side of a page. This space can be increased or decreased as necessary. This can also be

the location where elements such as headers and footers are located.

Merge   A feature that enables you to combine information, such as names and addresses, with a form document, such as a letter.

Mixed cell reference   A single cell entry in a formula that contains both a relative and an absolute cell reference. A mixed cell reference is helpful when you need a formula that always refers to the values in a specific column, but the values in the rows must change, and vice versa.

Negation   This is making a number a negative number.

Noncontiguous range   This is a range of cells that are linked together with the Ctrl key on the keyboard, but that are not necessarily in a straight row or column.

Object   Any element (workbook, chart, picture, and so on) that can be linked or moved in your workspace.

Office Assistant   An animated Office Help system that provides interactive help, tips, and other online assistance.

Operator   This is an item that is used to perform a calculation in a formula or function.

Overtype mode   A setting that makes new text you entered replace the text that was previously in the same location.

Page setup   The way data is arranged on a printed page.

Path   A way of identifying the folder that contains a file. For example, My Documents\Letters\Mom.doc means the document Mom.doc is stored in the Letters folder, which is stored in the My Documents folder.

Personalized menus   Menus that change to show the commands you use most often and adapt as you work.

PIM   Personal Information Manager. Software (such as the Contacts folder in Outlook) in which you track information about contacts and keep notes on your interaction with those contacts.

Plot area   This is the area where the data from a worksheet is plotted in a chart.

Pop-up menu   See *Shortcut menu.*

Portrait   This is the tall view of a printout.

Precedents   These are the cell references that are linked together to make up a function or formula calculation.

Print area   This is the area you select in Excel to print only.

Program window   This is the application window.

Qualifier   This is an element that separates delimited fields. For example, quotation marks around imported or exported data in a file.

Range   A cell or a rectangular group of adjacent cells in Excel.

Record   This is a row in a data list.

Reference   A means for addressing something in a specified context. For example, in Excel, "AI" is a reference to the cell at column A, row I.

Relative cell reference   A reference to the contents of a cell that Excel adjusts when you copy the formula to another cell or range of cells.

Repeating titles   This is when you select a row and or column of headers to repeat on each page of a printed worksheet.

Replace   A command on the Edit menu you can use to replace text with different text automatically. This feature can also be used with codes such as tabs and paragraph marks.

Revision marks   This is another name for the tracked changes you see onscreen.

Row   A horizontal set of cells in Excel.

Ruler   A means for judging distances of where objects are in relation to the page. Appearing horizontally across the top of a page and vertically along the side of a page in Word, rulers also display page margins and tab settings.

Sans Serif   A class of fonts that don't have "tails" on the letters, such as Helvetica and Arial.

Scale   You can increase or decrease the scale of objects or worksheets in Excel in order to make items fit in locations.

Scientific notation   This is when you exponentiate large numbers to the power of I0. For example, 1,000,000 is actually I0 to the 5th power.

ScreenTip   Notes that display on your screen to explain a function or feature.

Search criteria   A defined pattern or detail used to find matching records.

Select   To define a section of text so you can take action on it, such as copying, moving, or formatting it.

Series   This is when data follows a typical pattern. For example, Ist Quarter, 2nd Quarter, 3rd Quarter, 4th Quarter.

Serif   A class of fonts that have "tails" on the letters, such as Times New Roman and Courier.

Sheet   This is also known as a worksheet.

Sheet tabs   These are the tabs that you click to move through the work-sheets in workbooks.

Shortcut key   A keyboard combination that provides quick ways to execute menu commands. For example, Ctrl+S is a shortcut key for File, Save.

Shortcut menu   The menu that pops up when you right-click an object. This menu changes according to the context of the task you are trying to accomplish.

Sort   A function that rearranges the data in a list so it appears in alphabetical or numerical order.

Source data   This is where the data originated.

Speaker notes   Notes that help you document and give a presentation in PowerPoint.

Status bar   A place at the bottom of each Office window that tells you information about your documents and applications, such as whether you are in insert or overtype mode.

Strikethrough   A font option that appears if the text is marked out with a dash mark (for example, ~~strikethrough~~).

Style   A named collection of formatting settings that you can assign to text. For example, the Normal style might use the Times New Roman font at 11 points with standard margins.

Subcategory   This is when you indent cells within a column to make the initial item in the list the main category.

Submenu   A list of options that appears when you point at some menu items in Windows 95 and in applications designed for use with Windows 95. A small, right-pointing arrowhead appears to the right of menu items that have submenus.

Subtotal   This is a feature in Excel data lists that enables you to calculate subtotals on grouped data.

Tab   An element that allows you to separate objects with a precise amount of space (such as one inch), something that using the spacebar can't do.

Tab delimited   These are the items between fields of data when importing and exporting data.

Tab stop   An element that you place in your ruler to enable you to add space and alignment between your tabs. For example, you could add a right-, center-, or left-aligned tab stop.

Table   A series of rows and columns. The intersection of a row and column is called a cell, which is where you type text and numbers.

Taskbar   This is the bar along the bottom portion of a Windows 98 operating system where the Start button appears.

TaskPad   In Outlook, a list of tasks that displays when you use the Calendar folder.

Template   Predesigned patterns on which documents and workbooks can be based.

Text wrapping   This is when text automatically flows to the next line below without having to force the text to the next line (carriage return/enter key).

Toggle   The process of turning an option switch from On to Off (Yes to No).

Trace   This means to follow along a formula or function to see where the cell references start and end. See also *Dependents* and *Precedents*.

Transpose   This means to flip information. For example, you can transpose column headers with row headers to read a worksheet differently.

Truncated This means to cut off or to shorten.

URL A Uniform Resource Locator is a link to an addressable location on the Internet.

Validation See *Data validation*.

Value axis This is the x-axis on a chart.

Web Also known as the World Wide Web; a hypertext-based document retrieval system with machines linked to the Internet. This enables you to view documents, especially ones that are graphical in nature.

Wizard This is a Microsoft element that walks you through a procedure with a set of steps that tell you what you need to do.

Workbook An Excel document that contains one or more worksheets or chart sheets.

Worksheet In Excel, the workbook component that contains cell data, formulas, and charts.

Symbols

commands

Data menu commands

F

Trace Dependents button (Auditing toolbar), 109

Trace Errors button, 109

Trace Precedents button (Auditing toolbar), 108

tracing

dependents, 109

precedents, 108

Track Changes command (Tools menu), 58-60

tracking revision marks, 58-59

transposing worksheets, 48-49

triangles (cell comments), 55

troubleshooting

error, 102

#DIV/0! error, 103

#NAME? error, 104

#REF! error, 106

#VALUE! error, 105

circular references, 107

Trace Errors button, 109

U

underline format, applying, 70

underlined terms (online help system), 16

Undo button (Standard toolbar), 43, 129, 140, 181

Unfreeze Panes command (Window menu), 36

unhiding cell columns/rows, 82

updating worksheet data, 121

URLs (Uniform Resource Locators)

adding to worksheets, 176

clicking in worksheets, 177

V

Validation command (Data menu), 136

validation error message, changing, 137

value axis (charts), 110

View menu commands

Header and Footer, 160

Page Break Preview, 154

viewing

workbooks

multiple workbooks, 26

Print Preview, 148

worksheets, 28

as Web pages, 175

W-Y

Web Page Preview command (File menu), 175

Web pages

saving worksheets as, 174

viewing worksheets as, 175

Web toolbar, 177

What's This? command (Help menu), 18

Window menu commands

Arrange, 26

Freeze Panes, 36

Remove Split, 37

Split, 37

Unfreeze Panes, 36

windows, resizing application windows, 27

Windows, Shut Down command, 19

wizards, Chart Wizard, 112-113

Word

documents

copying workbooks to, 166-167

linking workbooks to, 166-167

Open dialog box, 171

Z

Get FREE books and more...when you register this book online for our Personal Bookshelf Program

http://register.quecorp.com/

 Register online and you can sign up for our *FREE Personal Bookshelf Program*...unlimited access to the electronic version of more than 200 complete computer books — immediately! That means you'll have 100,000 pages of valuable information onscreen, at your fingertips!

 Plus, you can access product support, including complimentary downloads, technical support files, book-focused links, companion Web sites, author sites, and more!

 And, don't miss out on the opportunity to sign up for a *FREE subscription to a weekly email newsletter* to help you stay current with news, announcements, sample book chapters, and special events including sweepstakes, contests, and various product giveaways!

 We value your comments! Best of all, the entire registration process takes only a few minutes to complete...so go online and get the greatest value going—absolutely FREE!

Don't Miss Out On This Great Opportunity!

QUE® is a product of Macmillan Computer Publishing USA—for more information, please visit: *www.mcp.com*